Biographical Note
Name: **pastor** Faith Daniels
Place of Birth: Lagos, Nigeria

Pastor faith Daniel is Co-founder of the altar of grace and mercy for miracle ministry and the school of prophet and deliverance.

The altar of grace and mercy for miracle ministries is a devoted revival of the apostolic signs, an unlimited demonstration of the power of God through worship, and the word of God to deliver to the uttermost and Holy Ghost fire where you are trained in the power of the Holy Ghost.

I am a teacher, preacher of the word, counselor, mentor, builder of leaders, and prophetic deliverance minister.

As a business administration graduate, I am an entrepreneur, a kingdomprenurship coach, graphic designer, writer, gospel singer and composer, wife, and mother.

Why do you want to write this book?

This book is a comprehensive study book with a biblical reference to help you to understand the importance of your dream, which can affect the physical state of your life in many ways. This prophetic manual gathers life experiences of dreams in years of deliverance ministry to expose the night's secret.

This book will show you how to enforce satanic dreams in your life so you can live in the victory God intended for every believer.

No longer will you have to try to battle to a place of victory in your dream or have bad dreams once you see the authority that is yours in 'Christ JESUS.'

As a believer, you are seated in the heavenly places in Christ. So come up and sit in the heavenly places in the prophetic room where you belong.

Read this enlightening book and gain insight concerning:

- Your dream.
- Doors that need to be shut.
- Power overnight Raider.
- How to war against destructive dreams.
- Prayer point to activate your prophetic dreams.
- Sources of dreams.
- How to journal your dream.
- Biblical Interpretation of dreams.

Biblical Dream Interpretation and Victory over Bad Dreams

God Way of Blessing through Dreams

By Faith Daniel

City: Lagos, Country: Nigeria
Instagram : igbagbo daniel
Copyright : Faith Daniels
Cover Design: Faith Daniels & Amrita Mitroo

Publisher: Self-Publishing on Amazon by Amrita Author Summit

Dedication

To the youth of the present generation and their children.

To people who desire to understand the power of dreams and their interpretation.

To people who want to activate their God-given dream and also walk in the prophetic power in this generation, with the hope that you will go on to follow the prophetic directions and prayers in this book to move to your next level in manifesting your divine purpose.

To the human spirit, destined to greatness in its desire to expose the glory of the richness of the treasure of God's grace.

To the Source and Sustained of the apostles and prophets, the Omnipotent One, and my personal Savior, my love and my king, my redeemer. My Lord Jesus Christ!

Contents

Acknowledgement

I am forever indebted to God for his grace and power to be all glory in Jesus's name.

I am ever mindful of the unparalleled love, prayer, support, and patience of my wonderful husband; I love you so much and our children, and I am deeply thankful for their understanding, inspiration, patience, and faithfulness in reminding me that they are my number one support team.

To Amrita Mitroo, my gifted and diligent editor and advisor, who co-labored with me in delivering this book? Thanks for your patience, tolerance, and persistence in seeing that I maximize the potential of this book.

To our ministry partners: thank you for your support in making sure that this book is published for millions of people to understand the mysteries behind dreams; more grace and strength to you in all that you do in Jesus' name.

Preface

There are millions of individuals whose glory, virtues, career, destiny, marriage, ministry, and children have been uplifted and empowered by Ed through their dream life. While there are millions of individuals whose destiny has been reprogrammed, whose glory has been stolen, marriage, children, business, ministry, whose virtues have been reduced to nothing through dreams, and yet they are just living their everyday life thinking that it is the will of God.

The power of the norm is the curse of our society. The everyday trending meditation has also opened doors of many people's lives to their enemies, which is the source of their demonic dreams.

It seems like the world is designed to make some Christian comfortable with the kind of life they are living and the pattern of dreams they are having. What a tragedy!

A glance at history reveals that the individuals who impacted their generations and affected the world most dramatically were individuals who, because of a circumstance, pressure, or decision, challenged their natural life, stretched the boundaries to become supernatural through the power of the Holy Spirit, and violated the expectations of the wicked powers of darkness. Few great things have ever been done within the confines of the accepted norm.

In essence, history is always made by individuals who dare to challenge and exceed the accepted pattern of this world that dreams don't mean much.

- People who dare to fast and pray to experience a mountain top life of prophetic dreams.

- People who know that there are powers that work when men are sleeping, which are forces of darkness but to remain victorious, you need to be on fire for God and understand that the spiritual controls the physical.

Why follow a path when you can make a trail?

It is incumbent upon each of us to ask ourselves the following questions:

Have we become all we are capable of?

Have I experienced God in my dream before?

Have I, as a Christian, experienced the flowing blood of Jesus Christ and the living water in my dream? If not, you need to read this book and discipline yourself through consecration, purification, the fire of the holy spirit, fasting, and meditation of the word of God.

I believe it is our Creator's will and desire that we commit and dedicate ourselves to and determine within ourselves to understand the power of our dream and the things of his kingdom.

Once again, the questions are echoed:

Have I fully gotten an interpretation of all my dreams which have had in the past?

How have I been able to use these dreams to help others?

How is my dream life affecting my own life? Is it a positive or negative impact?

Have we settled for lack of prayer and his grace?

Have we done our best?

It will help if you come to grips with these questions because they are related to your fulfillment, your contribution to the human family, and the pleasure of your Creator. Your Creator has endowed you with immeasurable treasures; your dream has been given as a spiritual altar to receive from him.

Introduction

'God Keeps Secrets'

God is a secret keeper. He has secrets. When you have access to His secrets, they will bring you uncommon success. God's ways are higher than our ways. His thoughts are higher than our thoughts. You will get outstanding results when you know His secrets, whose thoughts are very high.

God knows all things and is willing to reveal beneficial things to you in your dream. God prosper people through instructions in their dreams, and He shows them how to implement this instruction. The more of His secrets you know, the more outstanding and resounding your success will be in life. Your dream is significant; God uses it to connect with all men. In dreams, secrets to overcoming all obstacles of life are revealed.

God keeps secrets, especially when it defies human logic. He keeps secrets, especially when HE knows that many don't pay attention to their dream, but in the end, it is time to pay attention to the information you are receiving in your dreams, and also, this is the time to know how to interpret your dreams according to the word of God.

- God declares that He **will** communicate through dreams and visions in the New Testament (Acts 2:17).

  'AND IT SHALL BE IN THE LAST DAYS,' God says, 'THAT I WILL POUR FORTH OF MY SPIRIT ON ALL MANKIND; AND YOUR SONS AND YOUR DAUGHTERS SHALL PROPHESY, AND YOUR YOUNG MEN SHALL SEE VISIONS, AND YOUR OLD MEN SHALL DREAM DREAMS.'

- The last book of the Bible, Revelation, is all vision! I was in the Spirit on the Lord's Day, and I heard behind me a loud voice like the sound of a trumpet, saying, **"Write in your book what you see."** (Rev. 1:10-11).

This book is full of information to guide you prophetically, and I pray that as you read this book, you will have a personal encounter by the grace of the Holy Spirit for transformation and dream empowerment in Jesus' name.

Chapter 1

Dream

Acts 2:17, In the last days, God says, I will pour out my Spirit on all people; your sons and daughters will prophesy, your young men will see visions, your old men will dream dreams.

Your placement in life depends on the number of secrets of God you know through your dream when you sleep.

There are many divine mysteries and divine secrets, especially when you position yourself to receive direction from God through your dream.

This is Acts 2:17, in the last days, God says, I will pour out my Spirit on all people; your sons and daughters will prophesy, your young men will see visions, your old men will dream dreams.

His promise of God and even now the covenant of this word is manifesting mightily in these end times.

This is our inheritance through Jesus Christ, our Lord's redemptive blood.

God declared that He **would** speak through dreams and visions in the Old Testament (Numbers 12:6).

Hear now my words: If there is a prophet among you, I, the LORD, shall make myself known to him in a vision. I shall speak with him in a dream.

God reveals dreams to you to draw you to himself. He keeps secrets and reveals them to you to help you be the head, not the tails. He keeps secrets and reveals them to His children so they can prosper and show forth his great and mighty power and glory.

What do we mean when we say dream:

Definition of the dream: (Webster's definition)

1) **a series of thoughts**, images, or emotions occurring during sleep

Had a dream about climbing a mountain
— compare REM SLEEP

2) **an experience of waking life** having the characteristics of a dream: such as
a) **a visionary creation** of the imaginations
b) **a state of mind** marked by abstraction or release from reality :

Dreams are your vehicle of revelation. It is a means of revelation and the central way God has chosen to communicate with you.

Through dreams, God can convey to you the destiny of your family, your nation, and your career. In these last days, dreams are part of a prophetic outpouring God's power upon His people. His mantle is also given to His people to part in many red seas. By the time a person is 60 years old. He would have slept for 20 years. One-third of a person's life is spent sleeping. Dreams are visions during sleep, and abandoning what occupies one-third of one's life is very risky.

The dream is a revelation to man of a portion of the activities of the spirit realm.

The dream is a spiritual monitor that tells you what is going on in your life in the spirit realm.

The revelation knowledge you need to overcome 94 percent of your physical and spiritual problems, including financial, marital, and ministerial issues, can be received in the dream.

To be informed is to be transformed.

This couple had been dating for some time, and the brother finally said he was ready for marriage and that they should start the process; unfortunately, the sister had just received a fresh baptism of fire of the Holy Spirit, which unlocked her spiritual dream and sensitivity.

On the day she was baptized, she had a dream about the marriage she was about to enter, seeing clearly that the brother whom she had been courting for some time is a big black bird in the Spirit which someone in their family to her witchcraft meeting and that if she Marty's this brother she will end up becoming a slave to the witch and not only that to have children will be difficult. The end of that marriage was that she kept praying, but nothing happened.

She woke up and went back to sleep again; she had the same dream; she was so troubled and terrified when she woke up .she decided to start fasting to get the interpretation of the dream, and God confirmed to her that the full of information about that marriage with thee brother was true though the brother is a Christian. To cut the story short, she did not marry the brother, and she received another piece of information about a brother she had not met whom God had destined her to marry. She prayed about the physical manifestation, met her true husband, and was happily married with children.

The lesson of this story is that the information she received transformed her life and saved her from making a terrible mistake that could have jeopardized her destiny. **May you receive the baptism of fire for a divine revelation dream in Jesus' mighty name?**

Your dream is your spiritual mirror showing you what you are and what is going on in your spiritual life.

Your dream.is your informative power.

Your dream is an altar of communication and a place to receive information from the spiritual realms.

Key Scripture:

"In a dream, in a vision of the night, when deep sleep falls upon men while slumbering on their beds, then He opens the ears of men, and seals their instruction." (Job 33:15-16)

This verse teaches that a dream occurs when deep sleep falls upon men. According to the Bible, a vision is something that happens when a man is awake, while a dream is something that occurs when a man is asleep. Some who study dreams say that we always dream when we sleep, but we only remember dreams right before we awake. This would fit with the Scriptures in several cases where men remember a dream that woke them up.

Dreams can appear to be very real. Sometimes you may even wake up mad, sad, or scared, yet you realize after a while that it was just a dream, and you settle down.

When we sleep, this happens;

1. Our ears are open (Job: 33:16)
2. Our minds are quieted
3. Our spirits never sleep (Psalm 121:4)
4. Our analytical skepticism is gone
5. To hide mystery for us to seek it out (Proverbs 25:2)

In his book Dream Language, **Jim Goll says, "Visions reveal God's nature while dreams often give us direction or reveal some part of God's plan".**

The Purpose of Dreams:

1. It leads to the Heart of the Father- dreams should draw us closer to the Lord as we journal and spend time prayerfully pondering the meaning. We are free from distractions when we are asleep, and our barriers are down. The Lord can speak directly to us through dreams when we are sleeping.
2. It awakens our walk with Him.
3. It imparts intercessory burdens.
4. It launches you into the ministry.
5. It brings healing.

Examples of those God has Communicated to in Dreams in the Bible :

1) **God warned ungodly kings and rulers through dreams:**

"But God came to Abimelech in a dream by night and said to him, "Indeed you are a dead man because of the woman whom you have taken, for she is a man's wife." (Genesis 20:3)

"And God said to him in a dream, "Yes, I know that you did this in the integrity of your heart. God, I also withheld you from sinning against me; therefore, I did not let you touch her." (Genesis 20:6)

2) God gave Jacob the ability to get wealth in his dream:

And it happened, when the flocks conceived, I lifted my eyes and saw in a dream, and behold, the rams which leaped upon the flocks were streaked, speckled, and gray-spotted.

Then the Angel of God spoke to me in a dream, saying, 'Jacob.' And I said, 'Here I am.' And He said, 'Lift your eyes now and see, all the rams which leap on the flocks are streaked, speckled, and gray-spotted; for I have seen all that Laban is doing to you. I am the God of Bethel, where you anointed the pillar and where you made a vow to me. Now arise, get out of this land, and return to your family's land." (Genesis 31:10-13).

3) God warned Laban not to do any harm to Jacob in a dream:

But God had come to Laban the Syrian in a dream by night and said to him, 'Be careful that you speak to Jacob neither good nor bad. (Genesis 31:24)

4) The Lord appeared to Solomon in a dream and imparted wisdom and an understanding heart:

"At Gibeon, the Lord appeared to Solomon in a dream by night; and God said,' ask! What shall I give you?" (1 Kings 3:5)

In verses 9-15 of this same chapter, Solomon asks God to give him an understanding heart (hearing ear) to Judge God's people and that he would discern between good and evil. God granted Solomon this as riches and honor, which he did not ask for. God also gave him a long life. When Solomon woke up, he realized it had been a dream.

5) The birth of Jesus was orchestrated and directed through dreams and visions:

Matthew 1:18-25 tells of when Joseph decided what to do about Mary, his fiancée. The scripture states that an angel of the Lord appeared to him in a dream, saying, Joseph, son of David, do not be afraid to take to you Mary your wife, for that which is conceived in her is of the Holy Spirit.

Also, the wise men and Joseph were divinely warned in a dream:

And having been warned by God in a dream not to return to Herod, the magi left for their own country in another way. When they had gone, behold, an angel of the Lord appeared to Joseph in a dream and said, "Get up! Take the Child and His mother and flee to Egypt, and remain there until I tell you, for Herod is going to search for the Child to destroy Him."
(Matt 2:12-13)

ACTION-PLAN SELF ASSESSMENT: 5 Questions

Q1)

Q2)

Q3)

Q4)

Q5)

Chapter 2

Types of Dreams

"The secret things belong to the Lord our God, but the things revealed belong to us and to our children forever, that we may follow all the words of this law." Deuteronomy 29 vs 29

1) **A Simple Message Dream**- no need for interpretation. These dreams are direct and to the point, and self-interpreted. Ex; Matt.1-2., Joseph's dream concerning Mary and Herod.

2) **The Simple Symbolic Dream**- Dreams can be filled with symbols. The symbolism is clear enough that the dreamer and others can understand it without complicated interpretation. Most time, God uses

symbols to communicate with us. Ex: Joseph's dream in Gen 37.

3) **The Complex Symbolic Dream-** this type of dream needs interpretive skill from someone who has the ability in the gift of dream interpretation or from someone who knows how to seek God to find revelation.Ex: Daniel 2, 4, and 8.

Discerning a God-Given Dream

The following are the 3 Sources where dreams come from:

This is very important. If you know these three sources of dreams, you will be able to identify God-given dreams and this deception of the enemy.

a) **Dreams from GOD**
b) **Dreams from your NATURAL MAN**
c) **Dreams from the DEMONIC REALM**

a) **Dreams from God Voice of God:**
- Righteous
- Loving
- Unto Salvation
- Full of mercy
- Humble
- Authoritative
- Without condemnation

Truth – agrees with scripture Life-giving
Luke 12:32 (NKJV)

"Do not fear, little flock, for it is your Father's good pleasure to give you the kingdom".

b) Dreams from our Natural Man:

1. Body Dreams:

Body dreams generally arise from and reflect some aspect of a person's physical condition. Body dreams often reflect physical realities. A person who is sick may dream of being sick. A person experiencing depression or grief may have dreams reflecting their state of mind. A woman may dream that she is pregnant because she is.

2. Chemical Dreams:

Known as hormone dreams, often they are a result of medications. They may also arise because of changing or abnormal hormone or chemical levels in the body. PMS, diabetes, hypoglycemia—these and similar conditions involving chemical imbalances can stimulate these types of natural dreams.

A woman became so frightened because of her dream. She had a fever, and it was very intense; in a dream, she saw people flying, animals talking, and the world and Jupiter connected. She woke up, and she slept again, this time in her dream she saw a lion and a baby playing when she woke up she became frightened and concluded in her mind that she saw heaven and she was in heaven probably she was going to die.

When I heard about the dream, I laughed, and she was surprised to see me laughing. I told her the dream was a chemical dream resulting from her condition and medication. I also informed her that whenever she is sick or on the drug, whatever dreams she has, she should not is due to the normal Al change and that she should plead the blood of Jesus Christ against it and command the dream to be nullified and be destroyed.

3. Soulish Dreams:

Soulish dreams are often simply our emotions expressing our needs or desires. They may speak to us about the need for sanctification in some areas of our life. One significant value of soulish dreams is that they can show us things about ourselves that we may otherwise fail to see when awake.

As the believer becomes conformed to the likeness of Christ and gains the mind of Jesus Christ, they will have fewer and fewer dreams that come from the soul.

- The Voice of the Flesh
- Self-seeking
- Promoting personal agenda Self-Exalting
- Full of insecurity & fear

c) Dreams from the Demonic Realm:

Dark Dreams:

1. **Dark in mood & tone:** somber, depressing, melancholy dreams; dreams where everything is a little out of kilter, where something indefinable seems wrong or slightly off center.

2. **Dark dreams** typically are dark with subdued or muted colors. Black, gray, and sickly shades of green are abundant in this type of dream.

3. **Dreams of Fear or Panic**

Most nightmares, especially childhood nightmares, fall into this category. Simply rebuke it and invite God's presence in. If they persist, you may want to ask the

Lord what the root of it is so repentance and healing can take place.

Equip your children with tools for fighting the Devil. Teach them to rebuke the Devil, fix their eyes on Jesus, speak His Word, and even go back into a dream to defeat the enemy and bring about victory!

4. Dreams of Deception:

These dreams create images, impressions & thoughts in our minds that assist us in turning away from God's truth and light into darkness and error.

Possible attack areas include Doctrine (beliefs), finances, sexuality, relationships, career choices, character, and identity.

Reject the dream through prayer and confess out loud that that is **not** who you are; instead, you are a righteous son/daughter of God who is full of the light of God.

The Voice of Satan:
- Accusative
- Violates the Word (or twists it)
- Leads people away from the Savior
- Leads people away from righteousness Deceptive – appeals to the flesh

- It brings death & destruction
- Brings the fruit of fear

Categories of Spiritual Dreams from God:

God's communication with man is creative beyond understanding and more far-reaching than we can comprehend! He can reach every part of our life through the means of dreams if He so desires through these categories,

- Dreams of Destiny & Calling
- Edification & Exhortation
- The revelation of God & Scripture
- Comfort
- Correction
- Direction
- Warning
- Instruction
- Cleansing
- "Self-Condition": Revealing the heart and where we stand before God.
- Spiritual warfare
- Creativity: inventions/new ways of doing things.
- Impartation
- Intercession
- Healing

- Courage & Strength
- Revelation: Word of knowledge, prophetic understanding.
- Deliverance.

One day, a woman was tired of a physical situation, so she decided to fast and pray until God revealed the secrets behind the problem and gave her deliverance. She eventually had an encounter with God in her dream because she refused to give up; in that dream, God took her to her Father's house, and after that, God brought her to the covens of the strongman in that house and showed her how the placenta of all the children born in that family are buried in the same place with the same demonic pattern. In this dream, she saw the demon in charge of this placenta and all the children of that family, including her. She then brought out her placenta from this demonic altar, and also God told her what to do, and she did it then the placenta destroyed and after she collected a book which contains the file of the journey of her life from the strongmen of that family.

God led her out of this covens with the book in her hand, and she woke up. Since that they, she was able to understand why all the children born in that family remained the same with no purpose, no glory, no financial blessings, and no success, and God delivered her. The book she received was the book of her destiny, and since that experience in her dream, she experiences a divine turn around physically. My prayer today is that you have the sacred spiritual dream you need to have in any of the categories I have listed above for your life to be celebrated and to become a solutions to many problems in this end time. May you receive it in Jesus' mighty name?

Personal Reflection

Q1.the dream have been having is it source from God or my flesh_____

Q2.the are the source of the voice I have always had in my dream. Is it God or the enemy_____?

Chapter 3

Category of Dreamers

Numbers 12:66 And he said, "Hear my words: If there is a prophet among you, I the LORD make myself known to him in a vision; I speak with him in a dream.

Bible Gateway:

There are different kinds of dreamers, and it is essential that you know this to know how to pray your way to a **'PROPHETIC ENCOUNTER'** for transformation:

1) Manipulated Dreamers:

Been under the manipulation of darkness; this type of dreamer sees their friends as their enemy and enemy as a friend in their dream.

2) The Night Visioners:

They only dream in the night

3) Occultic Dreamers:

These are the people who are constantly meeting dangerous figures in their dreams. They often find themselves in strange, mysterious places among the strange force.

4) Vagabond Dreamers:

These are people who always see themselves in different places, roaming about in the spirit world—other cities, states, wilderness, streets, etc.

5) Meaningless dreamers:

Those whose dreams seem to be meaningless always.

Those whose dreams are erased: people who don't remember their dreams when they wake up. They always say they don't have dreams just because there is a power that erases their dream each time they sleep. Some people under this category only have dreams once in two months or one month.

6) The Instant Manifestation Dreamers:

This kind of people, anytime they have dreams, manifest immediately.

7) The Permanent Dreamers:

These kinds of people always have dreams no matter the time, day, or night. No matter where they are. Whenever they sleep or doze off, they will dream no matter how crowded or noisy the environment is.

8) The Moon Dreamer:

They only have dreams when the full moon is out.

9) Prophetic Dreamers:

These are the people whose dream altar has been transformed into a divine revelation .they see are the receiver of divine instructions, and direction and secrets are shown to them in their dreams. They always have a divine encounter with God when they sleep. I pray that this will be your lot in Jesus' name.

How to receive a good dream;

A. Your Spiritual Antenna-

We have to be tuned in and ready to receive God's transmissions. Get ready and expect to receive.

B. **Power of the Blood of Jesus Christ–**

Hebrews 9:12: "and not through the blood of goats and calves, but through His blood, He entered the holy place once for all, having obtained eternal redemption."

C. **Pray in the Spirit-**

Jude 20: "But you, beloved, build yourselves up on you most holy faith, praying in the Holy Spirit." Praying in the Spirit refreshes us, stirs our faith, and creates an atmosphere where God's mysteries are spoken and revealed.

D. **Meditate on God's Word –**

Joshua 1:8: "This book of the law shall not depart from your mouth, but you shall meditate on it day and night, so that you may be careful to do according to all that is written in it; for then you will make your way prosperous, and then you will have success."

E. **Worship and Sing Praises-**

2 Chronicles 20:18-22: This scripture talks about the worshippers going ahead of the army and defeating the enemy by their praise.

The Drain to Dreaming:

a) **Are you at rest, or are you striving**? –

Isaiah 30:15- "For thus the Lord God, the Holy One of Israel, has said, "In repentance and rest you will be saved, in quietness and trust is your strength."

b) The spiritual **receptor must be clean**.

Ephesians 4:23-27, "Be renewed in the Spirit of your mind, and put on the new self, which in the likeness of God has been created in righteousness and holiness of the truth. Therefore, laying aside falsehood, speak truth to each of you with his neighbor, for we are members of one another. Be angry, and yet do not sin, do not let the sun go down on your anger, and do not give the devil an opportunity .this Bible verse is pointing to things which are listed below that make our spiritual receptor, which is our mind, will thought and emotion which is connected to our subconscious mind to be unclean.

1) **Worry this can affect your dream** - Ps. 37:8

2) **Anger**- this is a terrible Anointing in which all believers must ask the fire of the Holy Ghost to dry up it quench the fire of one's dream. Ephesians 4:26

3) **Lust**- this is a perverse lustful feeling that can block the flow of divine information
Romans 13:10-14

4) **Bitterness**- Hebrews 12:15

5) **Our daily Routine or schedule** - inconsistent schedules can hinder the flow and retention of revelation. We often do not believe that this is our fault, just due to the demands of life. Ask the Lord for His grace to help you work out your schedule and even alter it if needed. Set apart times for receiving from the Lord. Sacrifice releases power. Fasting can be used to soften our hearts and put us in a position for heavenly downloads.

6) **Mismanagement of information and lack of documentation.**

7) **Integrity** -.

Tomorrow's call does not give you authority today. There is a learning process of being called, trained, and commissioned. Don't distort the meaning of a dream out of your insecurity. Don't say more than God says or more than God said to say. Learn to pray and hold-wait for more revelation before you speak.

Other things that can hinder your dreams could be:

1) Distraction:

The scripture says to set our minds on things above and not on earthly things. We must set aside time to receive revelation away from distractions- cell phones, computers, TV, books, magazines, friends, and family.

2) Lack of information:

What does God have to say in His Word? God still speaks to us today. Too often, as Christians, we look to institutions, denominations, and uninformed people to get our theology rather than basing it on the Word of God. Wrong information and lack of information are a culture that allows the doubts of darkness to breed and remain. Hosea 4:6 states:" My people are destroyed for lack of knowledge."

3) Disbelief:

Many can't and will not hear the voice of the Holy Spirit in their lives because they do not believe God wants to speak to them. Disbelief can filter out God's love, care, revelation, and at times His empowerment. Remember that we serve an all-powerful, all-knowing God who has spoken, is speaking, and will continue to speak to His people. The scripture in Mark 9:23 states, "I do believe, help my unbelief!".

4) Worldly Songs and Movies:

We must be careful what we watch and listen to. We must not give place to the devil by listening and watching all the demonic symbols and signs in it, including some of the words spoken in it, which are real spells that can open a strange portal in one's life, and this is when a strange spirit gain entry it can affect dreams. Your eye, ear, mouth, and nose are gateways you need to guide it.

5) Manipulation:

The enemy can manipulate one's dream through spells, witchcraft, voodoo, etc.

6) Demonic Projection:

Demonic dreams can be projected into one's life while sleeping.

7) Demonic Food:

Most food is polluted; not only that, many foods are dedicated to Satan. Many foods are sacrificed to a certain force of darkness; once taken, it automatically initiates one and opens portals to the enemy to get in, which can affect your dream.

8) Strange Plantations:

There are personalities called evil hairdressers in the spiritual realm that evil plate hair on people's heads in the dream; as a result, the inner hard becomes affected, which also affects the Dreamliner too. Evil plantation, most time, also happens through the dream of eating; dreams this can affect or block one's dreams

9) House:

The kind of house you live in or your environment can affect your dreams. If the house you are leaving us has a strange covenant or an evil plantation, it can affect your dream. If your environment is dominated by witchcraft or people who create an evil altar for sacrifices, this can affect your dream. If their a graveyard around where you leave or in the house you are leaving which someone is buried, it can affect your dream life because that grave can be used as a legal entry into your dream realm by the enemy's. Leaving in an occultic house or living with an occultic people.

10) **Artistic Designs** or

Materials or objects like rings, waist beads, wristbands or chains, or necklaces that have strange portals or have been dedicated to demons in them in your house or you wearing can affect your dreams.

11) **Beauty products** or hair products that have been dedicated to darkness.

12) **Unrenounced** evil covenant.

13) **Initiation with the darkness** that has not been broken.

14) **Past traumatic experience** that has not been healed.

15) **Demonic Soul Tie:**

With past sex mate, relationship, demonic house you have once lived before or the past strange church you have once been to or soul tie with ancestral altars of father's house or mother's house or a place you visited in the past for strange sacrifice. If you don't break the soul tie it can be an open door for attack s in your dreams, and it can affect your dreams.

16) **Subconscious Realm:**

If you have once been an occultic person, engaged in witchcraft, medium or warlock, or any of the Demonic realms, and you acquire a high rank in there, please take this seriously as you need to do a deep deliverance in other for the powerful demon that has been walking with you in your past which is the one who gave you the ability to project or do any mysterious things which operate through your subconscious realm as a transport we into the dark realms you need to be cast out of his place and holy Spirit take over after you have received Christ that's if you have not dealt with it because it will continue to operate through your dream unconsciously to you. The powerful demon must be addressed even if you have destroyed the covenants.

17) **Demonic** symbols or signs in cloths or on house designs

Personal Reflection

1. What kind of dreamer am I?

_____

_____

_____

_____

_____

_____

2. What are the things that are affecting my dream?

_____

_____

_____

_____

_____

_____

3. How can I change that?

_____

_____

_____

_____

_____

_____

Chapter 4

Prayer to Unlock Your Dreams

"The heavens declare the glory of God; the skies proclaim the work of his hands. Day after day they pour forth speech; night after night they display knowledge. There is no speech or language where their voice is not heard". Psalm 19 vs 1

Enemies always try their best to make sure men don't remember their dream; they prefer to keep them blank, for people do not know what is going on with their lives in the spiritual realm. Most times do this for you not to have access to some great information that can accelerate your destiny, marriage, career, and calling.

I remember meeting a man some years back who knew he always had dreams, but when he woke up, he couldn't even describe or recall anything that happened in his dreams, and he would say I do have dreams, but I don't remember it, but this bothers him a lot, and when he came for counseling he asked for prayers because he believes it's not normal... He was given prayers to pray, and he prayed for seven days before three days, his dream life was restored, and since then, he has always remembered his dreams.

Another woman also complains about not remembering her dream that each time she wakes up, she always has pains in her private part as if someone had sex with her; after praying holy spirit asked me to give her a prayer point under to days the lord open Ed her eye, and she saw who was always coming to her in her dream to have sex with her which was her physical, biological father.

She noticed a strange item in her father's hand, which he used to cast a spell on her after he finished in other for her not to remember. In that dream, she received holy anger from the Holy Spirit; she took the demonic item, destroyed it, and beat her father in that dream till he fainted and she woke up. Physically her father became so I'll he asked her to come that he offended that she should forgive her beloved this was a terrible dream she had been having for many years but never remembered as a result of this her life has remained in a terrible state without marriage etc., but she decided that enough is enough which brings about the unlocking of her dreams for her to see what was going on. May you receive holy anger to possess your possession in Jesus' mighty name?

Many people have dreams, but when they wake up, they don't remember them again, and many don't even have dreams. You can correct that by unlocking your dream through these prophetic prayers.

What to do whenever you don't remember your dreams:

1) Worship in tongues immediately when you wake up.do this for at least three minutes.
2) Ask the Holy Spirit to bring back into your memory the dream you had...wait for him to do this.
3) Write it down!
4) Ask him for interpretations.
5) Awaken naturally. Alarms and such can shatter dream recall .....Put your alert off next time.

6) If you do all this and still don't recall your dream, pray these prayers for seven days. Especially before you sleep from 12 am to 3 am, use Psalm 25, Psalm 19, and psalm 24 daily.

- Worship God.
- Ask for forgiveness of sin.
- Plead the blood of Jesus Christ over your head.
- By the power in the name of Jesus, I command the heaven of my dream to be open by fire in Jesus' name.
- I command by fire powers that are assigned against my head ...erasing my dream destroyed by fire in the name of Jesus Christ.
- Every evil altar connected to my inner head break by fire in the name of Jesus Christ.
- I command the light of my inner head to receive revival fire in the name of Jesus Christ.
- You, the altar of my dream, receive revival fire in the name of Jesus Christ.
- You, my spiritual antenna, by the resurrection power of Jesus, receive restoration in the name of Jesus Christ.
- Every evil plantation in the land of my dream blocking my spiritual pipeline be uprooted by fire in the name of Jesus Christ.
- You, my retentive memory, receive revival fire in the name of Jesus Christ.
- I connect my inner head to the resurrection power of Jesus Christ.

- You the heaven that declares the glory of God iron upon my head and begins to declare the glory of God for my day and night in Jesus' name.
- Pillar of fire of God incubate my night in Jesus' name.
- Every evil altar speaking against my dream in the night break by fire in Jesus' name.
- Every spiritual cataract in my spiritual eyes by the resurrection power destroy in Jesus name.
- You, the altar of my dream, become the altar of divine revelation in Jesus' name.
- The anointing of prophetic dreams come upon me now in the mighty name of Jesus Christ.
- As of today, I shut the doors that have been open in the past by powers of darkness which they are using against my dream by the blood of Jesus Christ.
- You, my subconscious mind, by the power in the blood of Jesus Christ, be transformed in the name of Jesus Christ.
- Every door opened unconsciously by me that the enemy is using to rob my dream life. I command the enemy operating through these doors to be bound now and cast you out in the name of Jesus Christ. I shut these doors by fire, and I severe the link by the blood of Jesus in Jesus' name.
- Every demonic ladder, bridge, cord, or link that the enemy is using to reprogram my dream destroy by fire.
- Powers that are attached to my inner head, walking against me through the heavenly elements by the

resurrection power, I pull down your strongholds, and I command you to destroy by fire.

- Disconnect my inner head from any demonic cycle of the moon that's been used to control my dream life in Jesus' name.

- Anoint your head after these prayers with the oil you prayed with, and always anoint your head before you sleep.

Personal Reflection

1. How can I discipline myself every day to pray this prayer to unlock my dream?

   _____

   _____

   _____

   _____

   _____

   _____

2. Make sure you anoint yourself every night by covering yourself with the blood of Jesus.

   _____

   _____

   _____

   _____

   _____

   _____

Chapter 5

Dealing with Bad Dreams

Psalms chapter 4 verse 8 says, "In peace I will both lie down and sleep; for you alone, O Lord, make me dwell in safety.

Bad dreams and nightmares are dangerous in any person's life, and bad dreams, if they are not curtailed, can be detrimental to any person's life. God has given us the power to pray and ask him for whatever we want. And we must ask him to help us cancel out dangerous dreams that might wish to truncate our lives and future. Nightmares are, no doubt, very scary.

The best thing to do after having a bad dream or nightmare is to pray to cancel it and reverse every demonic influence and the demonic effect of the dream. You have to pray that God helps you to cancel it. Why? This is because dreams are more of a lens into the possible events of the future. So, if you have a bad dream, the best thing is to pray to cancel it. Because it means that the devil is planning something evil in his coven, which is dangerous; if you watch the devil and don't do anything to counter it, you could be walking on dangerous shredded glass pieces.

- Dreams are real, yet the bible is replete with prayer against bad dreams that can help your dreams.

- Bad dreams point to something bad happening to you now, or something evil will happen to you.

- Many bad events that occur in many people doesn't happen. God often gives warns through our dream, no matter who, be it an unbeliever or a born-again Christian, because we all dream when we sleep .in the bible, He spoke to many who don't even believe in him.

Example

- King Abimelech - Gen 20 - (Sarah & Abraham),
- Midian Army - Judges 7:13-14 - (Gideon's Victory) Pharaoh's butler and baker – Gen.40:5

- Pharaoh – Gen 41:1,5
- Nebuchadnezzar – Dan.2:1, 4, 36
- Pilot's Wife - Matthew 27:19
- Wise Men – Matthew 2:12

The following are some examples of bad dreams:

- Eating in the dream
- Flying in the dream Swimming in the river
- Breastfeeding in the dream Going to the village
- Writing exams in the dream
- Carrying firewood in the dream
- Seeing red things in the dream
- Going back to your formal school Counting dirty money or rough money in the dream
- Crying in the dream
- Sexual dream.
- Walking naked
- Attacked by animals
- Losing your Bible in the dream
- Seeing corpses.
- Dead relatives or dead
- Going back to your former school or a former house or taking again examinations that you have already passed
- Being shot in the dream
- Been locked up, and there is no way out

- Wearing a black cap
- Wearing rags
- Seeing yourself aimlessly visiting a market
- Swimming
- Working as an enslaved person in a form or as a house help
- Broken staff
- Broken altar
- Broken wristwatch
- Lost or stolen money
- Been in total darkness
- Dry tree or a tree been cut off
- Rotten fruit
- Spiders and cobwebs
- Been arrested by police
- Traffic
- Broken mic
- Loss of voice
- Lost or stolen keys
- Chain and leg
- Self-duplicate dreams
- Strange marriage and wedding rings
- Waist chain
- Hair has been cut off or uprooted, or shaved off.
- Hair Wigs
- Strange hand-making hair for you in your dream at the time

- Seeing yourself in your village and yet you are in the city
- Stopping in the dream
- Been chased by strange forces
- Been shot in the dream
- Been cut or attacked with knives
- Graveyard
- Coffins
- Body parts have been cut off or missing

The following are the simple interpretations for most common dreams:

- **Dreams of** Your **House:**

This one would easily rank in the top five most common dreams. The house normally represents your life, and the circumstances taking place in the house reflect the specific activities in your life. These dreams may reflect the church as well. Individual rooms of the house may represent specific things.

For instance, if the bedroom appears, the dream may have something to do with intimacy issues.

The bathroom may represent a need for cleansing. The family room may be a clue that God wants to work on family relationships.

- **Dreams of Going to School:**

These dreams often center on taking tests. The tests may be for promotion. Or you might find yourself searching for your next class-an indication that guidance is needed or a graduation has just occurred. You might be repeating a class you took before, possibly meaning that you have an opportunity to learn from past failures.

High School dreams may signify that you are enrolled in the School of the Holy Spirit (H.S. = High School = Holy Spirit). There are limitless possibilities. These are just a few examples. Interestingly enough, the Teacher is always silent when giving a test. Another thing to note is that the enemy often uses this dream to demote and also to delay or to stops promotion, so discernment is needed, but the most important thing to do is to take the dream to the Holy Spirit.

- **Dreams of Various Vehicles:**

These may indicate your calling in your life, the vehicle of purpose that will carry you from one point to another. Cars, planes, buses, etc., may be symbols of the type or size of the ministry you are or will be engaged in. That's why there are different kinds of vehicles.

Note the color of the vehicle. If it is a car, what are the make and model?

Observe who is driving it. Are you driving, or is someone else driving?

If someone else is driving, who is it? Do you know the person? Is it a person from your past?

If the driver is faceless, this may refer to a person who will appear sometime in the future or that the Holy Spirit Himself is your driving guide.

- **Dreams Concerning Storms:**

Storm dreams tend to be intercessory, spiritual warfare-type dreams. They are particularly common for people who have a calling or gift in the area of discerning spirits.

These dreams often hint at things on the horizon — dark, negative storms of demonic attack for prayer, intercession, and spiritual warfare, as well as imminent showers of blessing.

What kind of storm is it? Are there tornadoes involved? What color are they?

Tornadoes can indicate a change that is coming, good or bad. Also, tornadoes can indicate great destruction.

- **Dreams of Flying or Soaring:**

Flying dreams deal with your spiritual capacity to rise above problems and difficulties and to soar into the heavenlies. These are some of the most inspirational and encouraging tones of all dreams. When awakening from a drama where you fly or soar, you often feel exhilarated –even inebriated- in the Spirit.

Ascending-type dreams are more unusual yet edifying. Remember, we are seated with Christ Jesus in heavenly places far above all principalities and powers.

- **Dreams of Being Naked or Exposed:**

These dreams indicate that you will be or are becoming transparent and vulnerable. Depending on your particular situation, this may be exhilarating or fearful and could reveal feelings of shame.

Note: these dreams are not meant to produce embarrassment but rather draw you into greater intimacy with the Lord and indicate places where greater transparency is required. These dreams often appear during times of transition where you are being dismantled to be re-mantled.

- **Dreams of Condition of Your Teeth:**

Often, these dreams reveal the need for wisdom. Are your teeth loose, rotten, falling out, or are they bright and shiny?

Do you have a good bite? Are you able to chew your cud?

Teeth represent wisdom, and teeth often appear loose in a dream. What does that mean?

It may mean that you need a wisdom application for something you are about to bite off. The fear of the Lord is the beginning of wisdom.

- **Dreams of Past Relationships:**

This kind of dream may indicate that you are tempted to fall back into old patterns and ways of thinking. Depending upon who the person is in the dream and what this person represents to you, these dreams might also indicate your need to renew your former desires and godly passions for good things in life.

Seeing a person from your past does not usually mean that you will renew your old relationship with that individual. Look more for what that person represents in your life – for good or bad. A person who was bad in your life may represent

God's warning to you not to relapse into old habits and mindsets that were not profitable. On the other hand, a person who was good in your life may represent God's desire or intention to restore good times that you thought were gone.

- **Dreams of Dying:**

These dreams are not normally about the person seen in the dream but are symbolic of something passing away or departing from your life. The type of death may be necessary to note. Watch, though, to see if the resurrection is on the other side.

- **Dreams of Birth:**

Usually, these dreams are not about an actual childbirth but new seasons of purpose and destiny coming into your life. If a name is given to the child, pay close attention because that usually indicates that a new season for God's purposes is being birthed.

There are exceptions to this where an actual pregnancy and birth are going to take place.

- **Dreams of Taking a Shower:**

These are cleansing-type dreams (toilets, showers, bathtubs, etc.) revealing things being flushed out of your life, cleansed, and washed away. These are good dreams, by the way. Enjoy the showers of God's love and mercy and get cleansed from the dirt of the world and its ways. Apply the blood of Jesus and get ready for a new day!

- **Dreams of Falling:**

These dreams may reveal a fear of losing control of some area of your life or, on the positive side, that you are becoming free of directing your own life. What substance you fall into in the dream is a key to proper understanding. The tremendous primary emotions in these dreams indicate which way to interpret them. Falling can be fearful but can also represent falling into the ocean of God's love.

- **Dreams of Chasing and Being Chased:**

Chasing dreams often reveal enemies at work, coming against your life and purpose. On the opposite side, they may indicate the passionate pursuit of God in your life and you towards Him.

Are you being chased? By whom? What emotions do you feel?

Are you afraid of being caught?

Or maybe you are the one doing the chasing. Whom are you chasing? Why? Again, what emotions do you feel during the chase?

The answers to these questions and, particularly, the dominant emotions in the dream will often help determine the direction of its interpretation. Often the Lord appears in various forms, motioning to us, saying, "Catch Me if you can!"

- **Dreams of Relatives, Alive and Dead:**

Most likely, these dreams indicate generational issues at work in your life —both blessings and curses. You must discern whether to accept the blessing or cut off the darkness. This is particularly true if grandparents appear in your dreams, as they will typically indicate generational issues.

- **Dreams Called Nightmares:**

Nightmares are more frequent with children and new believers in Christ, just like calling dreams to do. They may reveal generational enemies at work that need to be cut off. Stand against the enemies of fear. Call forth the opposite presence of God's amazing love, which casts out fear; the fear has torment!

- **Dreams of Snakes:**

The snake dream is probably one of the most common of all the categories of animal dreams. These dreams reveal the serpent – the devil with his demonic hosts- at work through accusation, lying, attacks, etc. Other common dreams of this nature include dreams of spiders, bears, and even alligators.

Spiders and bears are two other major animals that appear in dreams that show fear. The spider, in particular, releasing its deadly poison, is often a symbol of witchcraft and the occult.

- **Dreams of Dogs and Cats:**

After snakes, the dog appears most common animal appearing in dreams. A dog in your dream usually indicates friendship, loyalty, protection, and good feelings.

On the other hand, dog dreams may also reveal the dark side, including growling, attacking, biting, etc. Sometimes these dreams reveal a friend who is about to betray you.

• **Dreams of Going through Doors:**

These dreams generally reveal the change that is coming. New ways, new opportunities, and new advancements are on the way. Similar to dreams of doors are dreams including elevators or escalators, which indicate that you are rising higher into your purpose and your calling.

• **Dreams of Clocks and Watches:**

Clocks or watches in a dream reveal what time it is in your life or the need for a wake-up call in the Body of Christ or a nation. It is time to be alert and watchful. These dreams may also indicate a Scripture verse, giving a more profound message.

Are you a watchman on the walls? If so, what watch are you on?

• **Dreams with Scripture Verses:**

Sometimes you may have a dream in which Bible passages appear, indicating a message from God. This phenomenon may occur in several ways: verbal quotes where you hear a voice quoting a passage, digital clock-type readouts, and dramatizations of a scene from a Bible, just to name a few. Quite often, these are watchmen-type dreams, dreams of instructions filled with ways of

The following are the ways as to how to cancel bad dreams:

Everything in the universe answers to the word of God.

He made the heavens and the earth with God's word, and with the same word, He's restoring and recreating the universe even today. (See Hebrews 11:3, NIV)

With His word, He rules the visible and the invisible world.

And seeing you are joint heir with Christ and that He has vested you with the power, authority, and prerogative to act in His stead through His name, you too now have the ability through His word to influence the visible and the invisible world.

You can order things around your world; you can change things as far as it concerns you and the happening in your world.

You can call things to be, and they will.

You can forbid things from being, and they will not happen.

How?

By the same word with which He created all things in the first place, that same word is in your mouth now. (See 2 Peter 3:7, NIV)

Yes, you can cancel bad dreams; all you need to do is to find scriptures to cancel bad dreams and then do it by declaring aloud those scriptures in the name of Jesus.

Are you ready to cancel bad dreams?

The following are scriptures to cancel bad dreams you can stand on to pray:

1. **Isaiah 54:17, KJV:**

No weapon formed against thee shall prosper, and thou shalt condemn every tongue that shall rise against thee in judgment. This is the heritage of the LORD's servants, whose righteousness is of me, saith the LORD.

2. Isaiah 54:15, KJV:

Behold, they shall surely gather together, but not by me: whosoever shall gather together against thee shall fall for thy sake.

Prayers

- By the covenants and the power of this word, I cancel, and I destroy the negative influence of these dreams, and I reverse and destroy every form of evil that has been concluded in this dream against me and my destiny in the name of Jesus Christ.
- I command by the power in the name of Jesus Christ and by the covenants of the word of God that created all things. I commend the altar of darkness used as the gateway into my life to back up this dream. I command it to break by fire in the name of Jesus Christ.
- All the bad dreams I have had in the past, I call you forth by the blood of Jesus Christ. I command you to destroy by fire in the name of Jesus .you shall. Not come to pass.
- I destroy every bad dream that the enemy is using to control my life and my destiny in the name of Jesus Christ

3. Isaiah 8:10, KJV:

Take counsel together, and it shall come to nought; speak the word, and it shall not stand: for God is with us.

4. Matthew 15:13, KJV:

But he answered and said, every plant, which my heavenly Father hath not planted, shall be rooted up.

- I command you to dream of backwardness planted into my life. I command you to be uprooted by fire and destroy.
- Every dream of stagnation programmed into my life I command by the covenant of this word be uprooted by fire and destroy.
- Every dream of untimely death planted into my life was destroyed by fire in the name of Jesus Christ.
- You the evil altar of evil dreams planted Into the heavenly realm against me, speaking against me, working against me break by the resurrection power of Jesus Christ and I use the sword of this word of God and the power backing it up to break and destroy you in Jesus name.
- Altar of bad dreams program into the air against me break by fire in Jesus mighty name. The demon backing it up by the blood of Jesus Christ I bind you,

and I pull down your strongholds and render you powerless over everything that concerns in. me in Jesus name.

- Curses and spells programmed into my life through dreams, program d into my marriage, etc. by the power of this word and by fire be uprooted out and be destroyed in Jesus' mighty name.

5. **Numbers 23:23, KJV:**

Indeed there is no enchantment against Jacob, neither is there any divination against Israel: according to this time, it shall be said of Jacob and Israel, What hath God wrought!

- I stand in the power of this word of God, and I command every witchcraft, spell, voodoo, divinations forged against me through this dream to be reversed and be destroyed by fire in the name of Jesus Christ, for it is written that indeed there are no enchantments against me, neither is there any divination against me (your name or business or children, etc.).
- I command the power of God of that backup this Numbers 23 vs. 23 to destroy the evil influence of this witchcraft dream in Jesus' name.

6. **Matthew 18:18, KJV:**
Verily I say unto you, whatsoever ye shall bind on earth shall be bound in heaven: and whatsoever ye shall loose on earth shall be loosed in heaven.

- O, your powers of unclean Spirit walking with me in my dream realms, I bind you. Now by the power in the name of Jesus Christ and cast you out of my dream realms in the name. Of Jesus Christ.

- Every unfriendly friend walking with me in my dream by the authority of this word and by the power in the name. Of Jesus, I renounce every strange covenant that attached my life with you. I command that covenant to break by fire, and I command by the power in the name of Jesus Christ every soul tie connecting us in the realm of the Spirit. I command it to break by fire in the name of Jesus Christ.

- I bind you, unfriendly friend, in Jesus' name I cast you out of my life, by the blood of Jesus Christ I command total separation now by the blood of Jesus Christ.

- Every familiar Spirit that is familiar with my experience and relationships operating against me in my dream, I bind you in Jesus' name.

- Every familiar Spirit familiar with my ancestral mistakes, sin, and covenant operating in my dream comes from my Father, mother, uncle, relatives, cousins, etc. I release the sprinkling blood of Jesus Christ against you. I commend the document you are using to destroy the blood of Jesus Christ. I command you now to be exposed and be bound in Jesus' mighty name.

- Every portal open by an unconscious covenant of my parent which familiar Spirit is using against me, I command you that familiar Spirit be arrested by fire in the name of Jesus Christ, and I cast you out of my life in Jesus name, and I shut this portal against you by the blood of Jesus Christ and severe the link by the blood of Jesus Christ.

- You spirit husband /spirit wife projecting yourself into my Spirit for sexual intercourse I break soul tie with you, I renounce my initiation with you which has been created by the sexual intercourse and sexual huge in the name of Jesus Christ. I command the demonic implantation through the sexual intercourse you have had with me. I command it to be uprooted by fire in Jesus' name. I command in the name of Jesus Christ what you have stolen from me through this sexual intercourse. I command you right now to return it in Jesus' name. By the resurrection power of Jesus Christ, now be arrested by fire in the name of Jesus Christ, cast out, and never return. I shut the door of my inner man against you and the doors of my body against you by the blood of Jesus Christ in Jesus' name.
- You can also use Psalm 24 against spirit spouse dreams.

7. Psalm 37:14-15, KJV:

The wicked have drawn out the sword and have bent their bow to cast down the poor and needy and to slay such as be of upright conversation. Their sword shall enter into their own heart, and their bows shall be broken.

- Every wickedness of the wicked assign against me by the power in the name of Jesus Christ and by the covenants of this word I command it to destroy in the name. Of Jesus Chris.
- You, this dream that has been assigned as a weapon of death, sorrow, downfall, etc., I command it to backfire in seven folds as a weapon of destruction to where it comes from in the name of Jesus Christ.
- I cancel every evil effect of these dreams in my life in Jesus' name.

8. **Proverbs 21:30, KJV:**

There is no wisdom nor understanding nor counsel against the LORD.

9. **John 8:44, KJV:**

Ye are of your Father, the devil, and the lusts of your Father ye will do. He was a murderer from the beginning and abode not in the truth because there is no truth in him. When he speaketh a lie, he speaketh of his own: for he is a liar and the Father of it.

10. **1 John 3:8, KJV:**

He that committeth sin is of the devil; for the devil sinneth from the beginning. For this purpose, the Son of God was manifested so that he might destroy the devil's works.

You can also pray this prayer point to cancel bad dreams.
Dreams give you insights into your past, present, and future.

So when you have a bad dream that could be God's way of showing you what Satan and his hosts of evil spirits are doing behind the scene (in the realm of the Spirit) against you.

But the joy of knowing what Satan is planning or doing against you is that you can pray against those evil schemes revealed in the dream and cancel or stop them in the name of the Lord.

So, God reveals to redeem.

You have the advantage because God has made adequate provision in His word – with a warranty that you can do something about those dreams.

The following are the More Effective Power Prayer against Bad Dreams:

- Oh Lord, my Father, I bind every evil force and power that is tormenting and e against me through dreams, in the name of Jesus. (See Isaiah 8:9-10).
- Father, in the name of Jesus, I take authority over evil dreams (mention the dream); I destroy its effect and nullify its power. And I shall not be harmed. (See Luke 10:19).
- Satan, I know your work, you have come to steal, kill and destroy, but in the name of Jesus, I stop you in your track. I declare that you cannot touch me, in Jesus' name. (See John 10:10).
- Lord, your word guarantees good sleep, so I declare that my sleep shall be sweet tonight. No evil force is permitted to come at me through dreams again, in the name of Jesus Christ. I fortify and sanctify my dream life by the blood of Jesus (See Proverbs 3:24).
- Lord, you have not given me the Spirit of fear; therefore, I resist every form of fear that Satan may want to instill in me through this dream, in the name of Jesus. Fear, I bound you, I come against you, I cast you out of my mind and domain right now, in Jesus' name. (See 2 Timothy 1:7).
- Lord, I declare that no weapon formed against me in and through this dream shall prosper in the name of

Jesus. I condemn the force behind the dream in Jesus' name. (See Isaiah 54:17).

- Every enemy that is coming against me through this dream be destroyed and scattered before me, in Jesus' name (See Deuteronomy 28:7).
- Lord, I know my wrestling match is not with humans but with an already defeated unseen force assigned against me in this dream. In the name of Jesus, so I destroy them, in the name of Jesus. I enforce the victory of the cross over them, in Jesus' name. (See Ephesians 6:12).
- Oh Lord, I declare that every wickedness the wicked has devised against me has gone down with the dream, in Jesus' name. Wickedness has fallen for my sake. (See Psalm 27:1-2).
- In the name of Jesus, I overcome evil dreams by the blood of the Lamb. I overcome the wicked forces behind the evil dream by the power of the Lamb's blood, in Jesus' name. (See Revelation 12:11).
- In the name of Jesus, I say to this evil dream, go, get out. I declare you shall not prosper; your effect and intended evil will never happen in my life. Begone, in Jesus' name (See Mark 11:23).
- Through the Spirit of the Lord, I raise the standard of the name and the blood of Jesus Christ against every evil dream. I lift the standard of the Word of God against you; you shall not prosper nor come to pass in my life, in Jesus' name (See Isaiah 59:19).

- Evil dream, the Lord did not ordain you nor command you; therefore, shall you not come to pass, in Jesus' name. (See Lamentations 3:37).
- Dream, Christ has redeemed and freed me from your curse and effect; you shall not succeed against me, in Jesus' name. (See Galatians 3:13).
- I declare that as the redeemed of the Lord, no divination, an evil omen, and spell through dream and any other means shall succeed against me, in Jesus' name. (See Numbers 23:23).
- Every association of witches and wizards against me through dreams shall not prosper. I destroy them, in Jesus' name. (See Psalm 118:12).
- Lord, as you have said, contend with those who are contending against me and take the glory, in Jesus' name. (Isaiah 49:25).
- I cancel every form of evil dreams that might want to manifest in reality in my life.
- You are canceled in the name of Jesus. Every evil nightmare that I dreamt of that wants to bring poverty into my life; I cancel it today in the name of Jesus.
- Every form of an evil dream that wants to bring evil afflictions and diseases into my life in one way or the other, dreams are canceled in the name of Jesus.
- Lord, I ask that you use your fire from heaven to destroy every evil dream and nightmare that might want to manifest in my life in Jesus' name.

- Every evil cat that keeps appearing in my dreams and wants to steal my dreams and glory is destroyed in the name of Jesus.
- Every evil plan that the devil is concocting in the demonic realm to unleash evil nightmares on me in my sleep shall not come to pass in the name of Jesus. Destroy their plans by fire in Jesus' name.
- Lord, I ask for fire to consume all the enemies that want to feed me food and drink in my dream in Jesus' name. I cover myself in the blood of Jesus as I sleep.
- Father in heaven, I ask for divine protection every time I go to sleep, to protect me from evil nightmares that might want to show their ugly heads in Jesus' name.
- I decree today that today is the end of evil and bad nightmares in my life in Jesus' name. I send out the Holy Ghost to go out and destroy every evil plan and ploys of the enemies against me.
- Every spiritual husband or wife the devil uses to fight me, let them be destroyed today in Jesus' name.
- Lord, I ask for divine deliverance from every form of nightmare. Nightmares shall not have a place in my life in the name of Jesus.
- The Spirit of cleansing to purify my Spirit from all sorts of evil effects of nightmares and evil dreams, let such Spirit come into my life today in Jesus' name.

- I am cleansed today in Jesus' name.
- From today forward, I am delivered from the hands of evil dreams and nightmares.
- No weapon fashioned against me in the dream shall prosper in Jesus' name. Every evil arrow sent to me to attack me in my dream goes back to the sender in Jesus' name.
- Every evil dream trying to end poverty in my life is destroyed in Jesus' name.
- Every evil and wicked nightmare trying to pull me down in life, I rebuke you in Jesus' name.
- Every dream sent from the devil and his agents to destroy me in any way shall be destroyed by fire today in the name of Jesus.
- Every evil dream sent to me that doesn't want me to prosper in my academics, I rebuke you in the mighty name of Jesus.
- Every evil dream sent by the devil to inflict damage on my life goes back to the sender in the mighty name of Jesus.
- I cover my dream life in the blood of Jesus. I decree the blood of Jesus over every aspect of my life that the devil might want to use evil dreams to destroy.
- No weapon fashioned against my family in the form of evil dreams shall prosper.
- I decree that from today, I am free from every form of bondage that I have been placed in through devilish dreams.

- I refuse to eat any satanic food that the devil sent me in the dream. Every evil spiritual husband that has been sent to me in the dream to make love to me, I rebuke you in the mighty name of Jesus.
- Every spiritual wife or spouse that wants to make love to me in the dream.
- I bind you by fire. I shall not be a victim of eating in the dream again.
- I shall not be a victim of swimming in the dream in the name of Jesus.
- I shall not be a victim of breastfeeding in the dream in the name of Jesus.
- I shall not be an unfortunate victim of seeing dead people in the dream in the name of Jesus.
- I shall not dream of snails or slow-moving organisms in the dream in the name of Jesus.
- I shall not cook for a dead person in the dream in the name of Jesus.
- Every dream that wants to invite or bring sickness into my life, you are destroyed in the name of Jesus.
- Father Lord, I ask that you release your fire of wrath upon the devil and stop the nightmares I have been having.
- Every Spirit of black cats being sent to me in the dream, I rebuke it in Jesus' name.
- I shall never be a victim of nightmares again, in Jesus' name.

- From this day forward, I rebuke bad dreams in Jesus' name. By the blood of Jesus Christ, I cancel and destroy bad dreams, and I declare that I am free and delivered in Jesus' name from bad dreams and nightmares in my life.
- Thank you, God, because you have given me victory in Jesus' name .amen.
- Every confusion in my dream, my life is not your candidate, expire, in the name of Jesus.
- Arrow of disaster into my dream life, backfire in the name of Jesus.
- I cancel the effect of this dream_____(mention them), in Jesus' name.
- The blood of Jesus cancels every bad dream buried in my memory.
- Household witchcraft projecting the Spirit of bad dream into my life, receive the mysterious attack, in the name of Jesus.
- Every good dream that I have lost to the devil, I reclaim it back in the name of Jesus.
- Every spiritual attack from my dream waiting to be manifested, I cancel it by fire, in Jesus' name.
- Every power using my dream to pollute my life, marriage, finance, you are a failure, be destroyed in Jesus' name.
- Every spirit husband/wife tormenting me in the dream, catch fire, in the name of Jesus.

- Anyone in my family or environment that has vowed to trouble me in the dream die by fire, in Jesus' name.
- Powers from my environment that vowed that I would never have a good dream are you my God? Scatter by fire, in Jesus' name.
- Every power using my dream to monitor me and track my movement, fall and die, in Jesus' name.
- Every strange oppression from the department of my dream life backfire in the name of Jesus.
- Every dark power that has swallowed my glorious dream begins to vomit them and die, in Jesus' name.
- (Hold your head and say)." My memory, reject all kinds of bad dreams in the name of Jesus."
- Every power jingling the bell of affliction in my dream, I command you to run mad, in Jesus' name.
- Every power rejoicing at the negative side of my dream, let your joy over me turn to sorrow, in Jesus' name.
- Anywhere the enemy has submitted my names to that is bringing attacks in my dream, go back to the sender 100 times. Run mad.
- I paralyze and destroy all satanic dreams, both the one in my memory and the one that is about to be fired against me in the name of Jesus.
- O GOD OF JOSEPH, reveal this dream to me (mention it to God), in Jesus' name.

- Every practice of masquerade in my village, opening the ground for a bad dream, catch fire, in Jesus' name.
- I claim my glorious dream now, in Jesus' name.
- (Hold your organ and say) "My organ, hear the word of the Lord, become fire in Jesus name reject sexual manipulation in the dream, in Jesus name.
- I separate my life, my name, from the activities of night attackers, in Jesus' name.
- I cancel all enchantments against me, in Jesus' name.
- Every power using curses to put a **full stop** to my destiny, receive the fire of God, in Jesus' name.
- I bind every Spirit of death and hell fired into my dream, backfire 21 times in Jesus' name.
- I withdraw my names from the list of people that are supposed to die this year.
- I withdraw any form of my personal belongings that represents me in the dark world, in Jesus' name.
- Spirit of dog programmed into my destiny, jump out, in Jesus name.
- Spirit of serpent programmed into my dream, fly out, in the name of Jesus.
- Spirit of loss, against me, be converted to an abundance of wealth, in Jesus' name.
- Wherever I have missed the roadmap of my destiny, I receive divine direction, in Jesus' name.

- Every power drinking the blood of my pregnancy and milk of my breast, I am no more your candidate, die, in Jesus' name.
- (Put your names if you can), you will achieve your divine destiny and make faster progress. No matter the manipulation against you, I shall rise and shine to the world, in Jesus' name.
- My Father, as of today, I am a candidate for a good dream, in Jesus' name.
- Every power hindering my angel of destiny from locating me in the dream, clear away by fire, in Jesus' name.
- Every bad dream that is about to add sorrow and disappointment into my life, I reject you by fire, in Jesus' name.
- Every spiritual food I have eaten from the devil's table, I vomit it out in Jesus' name. (Drink a little anointing oil as the form of blood of Jesus).
- O God, whoever is plucking my fruit of glory from my dream, I challenge you today, hand it over to me and die, in Jesus' name.
- I reject the Spirit of backwardness and slow progress; in Jesus' name.
- Blood of Jesus, wash me thoroughly and protect me, in Jesus' name.
- (For man only), My sperm stole by any strange woman, both in the physical or spiritual, I repossess it back by the fire, in Jesus' name.

- (For man only), My wealth stolen by any strange woman in the dream and physical, I repossess it by fire, in Jesus' name.
- Let all strange dreams that I am used to beginning to fall out from my dream life in Jesus' name

Personal Reflection

1. I identification of prayers against feeding in the dreams
2. Prayers against sex in the dream
3. Prayers to reverse every evil dream that is working against your life.

Write it out and pray it out loud to

_____

_____

_____

_____

_____

_____

_____

_____

_____

_____

_____

_____

_____

_____

_____

_____

_____

Chapter 6

How to Journal your Dream

Habakkuk 2:2
NRSV
2 Then the Lord answered me and said:
Write the vision;
make it plain on tablets,
so that a runner may read it.

Recording and Interpreting Your Dreams:

For you to wake up with divine information and remember it is a sacred gift from God and that's is just because He believes in you that he can trust you with secret information, so you must thank him constantly for that and not only that for him to know that he can trust you with more information is when you begin to journal it by writing in details what you have received.

In my journey, I love writing about many things I receive from God; not only that, I love detailing them because of future reference. Though most of the time, laziness may want to step in, I keep it simple by writing out the necessary information and let me tell you, this detail has been like a life rescuer in many ways in this ministerial journey.

A sister who has an intercessory ministry, in which God always shows solutions to people's problems before she meets them. She has a dream one night about a child who has had an issue, and in that dream, she saw herself praising God on behalf of this child for his healing and the whole family was confused, because the child was sick and nothing seems to be working concerning the head issue. She just kept on giving thanks, and before their very eyes, the head of the boy was restored in that dream, and she woke up.

She wrote the dream down in her journal, and after a long time, she met this person whom she dreamt about, and she had total forgotten about it, but she started interceding on behalf of the child and the parent; after a while, she then saw the dream in her journal when she was going through it. She did exactly what she did in that dream which praised God, and the child received his healing. Imagine if that dream were not documented with divine instruction she received, that child would have just remained sick or probably died. This is why it is essential to write out your dream because it may save someone's life one day.

It all starts with one step, decision, discipline, and commitment:

1. Name, date, title your dream, and record your waking time. Daniel 7:1,"...Daniel had a dream and visions of his head while on his bed. Then he wrote down the dream, telling the main facts."

2. Write or draw your dream in bullet points, diagrams, outlines, or paragraph form.

3. Record the main facts and eliminate the unnecessary details

4. Ask the Holy Spirit for insight and understanding of the dream.

5. Does the dream symbol appear in the Bible? Search it out in Word. Dreams from the Lord will never go against His Word. (Prov. 25:2)

6. Ask questions about what you saw in your dream. What did you sense and feel from the dream? Was it a good or evil presence, fear, love, concern, hopelessness, or disappointment? What was the primary emotion? What are the colors? Is everything in black and white or color? (Zechariah 4)

7. Look for the theme or essence the dream is communicating to you. Relate the dreams to your circumstances and spheres of influence. Consecutive dreams often have the same or similar meanings. (Gen.41:1-7, 25-31). God will speak the same message more than once.

8. Keeping it simple is better than trying to complicate the dream. Most times, you may even feel so tired of writing one that you get the significant message out; it saves you from stress

9. Visualize the dream as you recall or rehearse the main symbols in the scenes of the dream.

When understanding and interpreting dreams, remember that our Heavenly Father has given us a Helper and will reveal the truth. All we have to do is ask.

"But the Helper, the Holy Spirit, whom the Father will send in my name, He will teach you all things, and bring to your remembrance all that I, said to you." (John14:26)

"But when He, the Spirit of truth, comes, He will guide you into all the truth; for He will not speak on His initiative, but whatever He hears, He will speak; and He will disclose to you what is to come. He will glorify me, for He will take of mine and will disclose it to you. All things that the Father has are mine; therefore, I said He takes of mine and will disclose it to you."
(1 John 16:13-15)

"But if any of you lacks wisdom, let him ask of God, who gives to all generously and without reproach, and it will be given to him. But he must ask in faith without any doubt, for the one who doubts is like the surf of the sea, driven and tossed by the wind. For that man ought not to expect to receive anything from the Lord, being a double-minded man, unstable in all his ways."
(James 1:5-8)

Prayers for Good Dreams to Manifest:

God must have shown you things in dreams; some of them are a revelation of what Satan is up to in your life and family, and others reveal God's plan and purpose and what He's doing in your life at the moment – what is happening in your life now so has you journal your dream down is important you pray for the manifestation of that dream.

Whatever the dream, God reveals to redeem, He reveals to warn, show direction and give instructions.

You have the power and authority to empower good dreams to manifest in the name of Jesus and also to conceal bad dreams.

Prayers for Good Dreams to Manifest:

The following are prayers for good dreams to manifest; you can pray these prayers every time you see something good in your vision about your life, family, ministry, and business:

1. Pray and thank God for revealing His plans to you

For God does speak—now one way, now another—though no one perceives it. In a dream, in a vision of the night, when deep sleep falls on people as they slumber in their beds, he may speak in their ears and terrify them with warnings, to turn them from wrongdoing and keep them from pride, to preserve them from the pit, their lives from perishing by the sword. (Job 33:14-18, NIV).

2. Pray and commit the dream back into the hands of God because He alone has the power to cause a dream he showed you to manifest.

3. Pray and ask the Lord to open up every detail of the dream to you, in Jesus' name.

4. Ask the Lord to send forth His ministry angels to see to the working out of every detail of the dream, in Jesus' name.

And then shall he send his angels, and shall gather together his elect from the four winds, from the uttermost part of the earth to the uttermost part of heaven. (Mark 13:27, KJV).

5. Pray and release the blood of Jesus upon these dreams for the good and manifestation of the dream, in Jesus' name.

And we know that all things work together for good to those who love God and those who are called according to his purpose. (Romans 8:28, KJV)
6. Pray and ask the Lord to shake everything that must shake and break everything that should break for the dream to manifest, in Jesus' name.

7. Pray and ask the Lord to level every mountain that must be leveled and fill every valley that should be filled for the manifestation of the dream, in Jesus' name.

Every valley shall be exalted, and every mountain and hill shall be made low: and the crooked shall be made straight, and the rough places plain: And the glory of the LORD shall be revealed, and all flesh shall see it together: for the mouth of the LORD hath spoken it. (Isa 40:4-5, KJV).

8. Pray and ask the Lord to order your steps in the direction of the manifestation of the dreams, in Jesus' name.

9. Pray and ask the Lord to cause you to make the right decisions and make the right moves required to manifest your dreams, in Jesus' name.

10. Pray and ask the Lord to drive you by His divine invisible hand of power so you will be at the right place and at the right time with the right people for the manifestation of the dream, in Jesus' name.

Order my steps in thy Word: and let not any iniquity have dominion over me. (Psalm 119:133, KJV)

11. Pray and ask the Lord by the mighty of the holy Spirit and his Anointing, the dream be activated and manifest without any delay to the glory of God in Jesus' name

12. Pray and ask the Lord to create the circumstances that will make for the manifestation of the dream in Jesus' name.

Personal Reflection

1. Write out that first dream that comes to mind that you have had in the past?

_____

_____

_____

_____

_____

_____

_____

2. What was the dream all about? Write the detail only?

_____

_____

_____

_____

_____

_____

_____

3. Put the dates and months, then close it and anoint yourself for the activation of that good dream?

_____

_____

_____

_____

_____

_____

_____

_____

Chapter 7

How God Appears in Dreams

In the beginning was the Word, and the Word was with God, and the Word was God. (John 1:1).

God reveals himself to his people, each Trinitarian person to the other two, and his revelation extends beyond his being. It also comes to the world he has created, especially the intelligent creatures of that world: angels and human beings. Because self-revelation is his nature, he wants all his creatures to know him.

God makes himself known to his creatures because he first knows himself perfectly as a personal, speaking God. Although all people suppress the knowledge of

God in their sin, he has communicated about himself to his creatures through creation, and human beings are made in God's image. On top of this general revelation, God communicates about himself to particular people in special revelation.

John m.frame.

As God the father

Earthly father
Protective figures: policeman, Army Sergeant,
Rich man
Spiritual father or leader
Governor

As God the son

Bridegroom
Savior/rescuer: someone intervening to bring you to safety.
Natural Ruler: Governor, King, Prime Minister, etc.
Fisherman
Carpenter
Shepherd
Warrior
Spiritual Leader
Lion

Pastor

Lawyer: defending you or acting as an advocate on your behalf.

Judge

Lover

Doctor (great physician)

As God the Spirit

Wind, Wine, Water, Fire

Faceless man with a light countenance

Counselor: someone giving you advice and counsel

Guide: a person is showing the right way to go.

Comforter: someone bringing peace and comfort to you.

Giver of Gifts

Coach

Captain

Personal Reflection

1. Have you ever had an encounter in your dream that reflects the character above?

_____

_____

_____

_____

_____

2. If yes, what were your feeling in the dream?

_____

_____

_____

_____

_____

3. Now that you know how God appears, Go ahead and thank him and ask for his encounter in your dream

_____

_____

_____

_____

_____

Chapter 8

The Information Room of the Holy Spirit.

"After this I looked, and there before me was a door standing open (A) in heaven. And the voice I had first heard speaking to me like a trumpet (B) said, "Come up here,(C) and I will show you what must take place after this". Revelation 4 vs 1

There is a place you must enter. A room is designed for you to dwell when you enter this place; your dream becomes a PROPHETIC dream. This place is non-negotiable to all Christian. You must get there if you desire the same grace upon the prophet and the apostles.

Many Christians had the wrong idea about the importance of the Holy Spirit. They understood the Spirit's role in their conversion, but they are missing out on his role as Helper in the ongoing life of a believer. Their new life in Christ had begun by responding to the Holy Spirit through faith, but they were now trying to maintain it by human effort; rather than relying on him in the aspect of the spiritual realm, they relied on another source. Some can't sleep without listening to a worldly song, comedy, or nonbiblical spiritual meditation instrument. They will say it helps them to sleep, but the truth of the matter is such a person's life is opened up to strange forces, inspirations that are not from God, and initiation with powers of darkness.

If you have been having bad dreams and also nightmares, it can be transformed.

If you usually experience demonic summoning while you sleep, there is a place you need to be translated into the secret place of the highest good. The information room of divine revelation.

- A place where deep secrets are revealed and where solutions are given.

- The information room is the place of divine protection where you are protected from forms of spells, voodoo, demonic incantation, etc.
- It is a place of power and authority.
- It is a place of divine guidance.
- It is a place of shekinah glory of God that no darkness can operate.
- It is a place of victory.
- It is a place of the mercy of God that abort and avert all judgment of darkness.
- It is a supernatural place of God.
- It is a place of experience of the word of God has it is in the Spirit.
- It is a place of solution for hard situations.
- It is a place of shelter.
- It is a place of provision.
- It is a place of prophetic grace.
- It is the upper room of God.
- This is a place of manifestation of good dreams, your Joseph dream.
- It is also the place of the word of God.

Many Christians today get caught with many things: we forget why the Holy Spirit is so important. If we want to avoid being "ignorant," we must thirst to dwell in this secret place, in this informative room of the Holy Spirit.

The following are five key roles that the Holy Spirit plays in this upper room experience:

1. HE GUIDES YOU INTO JESUS' TRUTH:

Jesus was clear on the importance of the Holy Spirit: "But when he, the Spirit of truth, comes, he will guide you into all the truth... he will glorify me because it is from me that he will receive what he will make known to you" (John 16:13-14).

Do you want to know what Jesus is saying to you as you journey through this life?

Do you want to hear God's voice as you sleep?
The Holy Spirit, the Spirit of Truth, communicates all of that to you in your dream.

2. HE DIRECTS YOUR STEPS:

The Holy Spirit not only speaks the words of Jesus to you, but he is the One who leads and directs your steps into the abundant life that Jesus promised. Paul wrote, "You are controlled not by the sinful nature but by the Spirit.... And if the Spirit of Him who raised Jesus from the dead is living in you, He who raised Christ from the dead will also give life to your mortal bodies through his Spirit, who lives in you" (Romans 8:9, 11).

The Holy Spirit is the conduit of life from God into your heart. He is the One who controls your thoughts, attitudes, words, and actions as you follow his lead in your subconscious realm as you sleep. He will direct your steps through all the complicated paths and speak the right word for any situation in your dreams.

Why am I saying this? Some people can speak in tongues while awake; they can prophesy, but when they dream, the enemy attacks them, and they are powerless.

A sister had a dream some years ago, in that dream she had an attack and there was this person that came, and she wanted to call the name of Jesus Christ but she could not, and also she says a Bible verse against this powers that came to attack her but she could not, and she woke up.

Another time she had an encounter again in another dream, the enemy came, and they beat up very bad each time she tried to call the name of Jesus Christ, they would slap her mouth and ask her to keep quiet. The enemy messed her up.

When she woke up, she was tired all her body was in pain. She was embarrassed to tell anyone because of her post in the Church. she eventually heard about the baptism of fire of the holy Spirit and dwelling in the information room of the Holy spirit she was thirsty and hungry for this experience, so she fasted for days and prayed until she received the baptism of fire and translated into the secret place of the highest God the. Her dream life changed.

In the next dream she had after her encounter, the enemy came as usual, but this time when they tried to attack her, she called on the fire of the holy ghost, and it consumed them immediately since that night, her dream became a place of divine information and visitation of God.

As you read this, I pray that you experience God's secret place in Jesus' name.

3. HE GIVES YOU SPIRITUAL GIFTS:

The Holy Spirit is also the One who gives spiritual gifts to all followers of Jesus so that we all can play our role in the Body of Christ. Paul gave us a sampling of those gifts in his first letter to the Corinthian Church:

"Now to each One, the manifestation of the Spirit is given for the common good. To one there is given through the Spirit a message of wisdom, to another a message of knowledge by means of the same Spirit, to another faith by the same Spirit, to another gift of healing by that one Spirit, to another miraculous power, to another prophecy, to another distinguishing between spirits, to another speaking in different kinds of tongues, and to still another the interpretation of tongues. All these are the work of the same Spirit, and he distributes them to each one, just as he determines" (1 Corinthians 12:7-11).

It is through these gifts of the Spirit that we function best as the Church, and it is through these gifts that we can proclaim the power of Jesus to people who desperately need to know our Savior physically and spiritually against the power of darkness even when we are unconscious to our physical environment. At the same time, we sleep. Spiritual gift is not only for when you are conscious, but they should be more active in your subconscious mind. My prayer for you is that your level of fire of the Holy Spirit should be increased in Jesus' name as you experience this information room in Jesus' name.

4. **HE EMPOWERS YOU TO PROCLAIM:**

A Lot of Christian physically can quote Bible verses and also do it boldly, but when they sleep, they are ridiculed by the powers of darkness in their dream. Their physical energy does not match their subconscious energy, which is connected to their spiritual man. However, when you enter into his secret place, when you enter into this upper room, into the information room of power of the Holy Spirit, you will be empowered to proclaim and also to command the power of darkness to be silent both physically and spiritually, especially in your dream realm.

In Acts, Luke recalls the crucial role of the Holy Spirit in the early Church's proclamation of the Gospel. When Peter and John stood accused before powerful leaders, Luke reported that Peter was filled with the Holy Spirit and boldly proclaimed that Jesus Christ of Nazareth, the One they had crucified, was the only way to salvation (Acts 4:5-12).

This is the same Peter who only two months earlier had denied Jesus. And now, standing in the very place where Jesus had been condemned, Peter accused this religious elite that they had crucified the Messiah. That new boldness could only be possible through the empowerment of the Holy Spirit. Christians need this boldness physically and spiritually when the enemy comes against them. Holy Spirit, give you that heat of the lion of the tribe of Judah to possess your possessions.

5. HE GUARANTEES YOUR HOPE IN HEAVEN:

The Holy Spirit is also important because he is the guarantee of your inheritance in heaven. "When you believed, you were marked in him with a seal, the promised Holy Spirit, who is a deposit guaranteeing our inheritance until the redemption of those who are God's possession" (Ephesians 1:13-14). Satan wants to destroy your hope and tries to get you to doubt your Savior's love. But the Spirit's leading, teaching, gifting and proclaiming prove that you belong to God forever.

So don't let anyone "bewitch" you. The Holy Spirit is of vital importance in your life. It is through him that the character of Christ is revealed in you: "The fruit of the Spirit is love, joy, peace, forbearance, kindness, goodness, faithfulness, gentleness and self-control which purified your heart and a symbol of the garment of righteousness on your inner man in the spiritual realms. This pure identity is a weapon against strange Demonic dreams and darkness. Against such things, there is no law…. Since we live by the Spirit, let us keep in step with the Spirit" (Galatians 5:22-23, 25)

Personal Reflection

What to do:

- Surrender yourself to God,

- Surrender yourself totally to Holy Spirit.

- Dedicate the altar of your dream to God.

- Ask the fire of the Holy Spirit to incubate it and transform it into the revelation altar.

- Separate yourself for personal encounters through fasting and prayer as God translates you to his secret place according to psalm 91 vs. one, which has the power of the Holy Spirit to seal you up with fire from today against evil summoning in Jesus' name.

- Ask for God to overshadow you and translate you into the upper room of the Holy Spirit, the secret place of the highest good, the information room for divine encounters every time you sleep. The place where the apostles and prophets dwell is the room of power.

Chapter 9

Interpretation of People in Your Dream

Genesis 40:8

8 They said to him, "We have had dreams, and there is no one to interpret them." And Joseph said to them, "Do not interpretations belong to God? Please tell them to me."

Bible Gateway:

Joseph was a man with a gift of Interpretation of dreams, and also Daniel, this gift is from God.

Daniel was a man of dream and gift of Interpretation. Lord blessed him with the gift of interpreting dreams and visions. This endowment soon made him an object of greater attention from the emperor, and he was raised to positions that enabled him to spend his life in service to the kings of the land. He became the Lord's ministry to those rulers.

Daniel 2:28 reads: 'there is a God in heaven who reveals mysteries:

There is more behind the scenes than we usually see; a cosmic conflict is raging that affects events on earth; but in dreams, God reveals what is going on. Chapters 2 and 7 contain prophetic dreams – an uncongenial idea in secular western culture but very familiar in most cultures. Daniel's Interpretation of Nebuchadnezzar's dream (chapter 2) and his dream (chapter 7) and the Interpretation he gives according to the grace of Interpretation given to him by God tells us that Interpretation is of our God. He alone is the one who can give the divine and exact meaning h or Interpretation of dreams.

Daniel 2:26–30. "There Is a God in Heaven That Revealeth Secrets":

Though the king would have given Daniel credit for providing the Interpretation of his dream, Daniel made it clear that it was not he, nor any of the wise men or soothsayers, who could determine the nature of the dream and its Interpretation. Daniel testified that "there is a God in heaven" (Daniel 2:28), and the secret of Nebuchadnezzar's dream was made known by the power of that God. Daniel did not take credit for himself for what the Lord had done for his benefit. The gift given to Daniel that made him a great man respected by the king and emperor is still very available for many that for it. You also can become gifted as Daniel in this generation.

The question is, are you ready and hungry enough to ask for it from God? The Interpretation given below is according to biblical meaning and interpretations. Above all, pray this prayer.

Father, the anointing of the divine gift of Interpretation of dreams and vision I ask for in my life that it rests upon me has from today in Jesus' name as I study this Interpretation in Jesus' name.

Baby:

New birth; barren women pitied; reproductive; ministry in its infancy stage; helpless; new Christian;

baby Christian; new move of God; spiritual immaturity; reward; fruitfulness; new covenant; a miracle. (1 Corinthians 3: 1; Gen. 21: 6; 1 Sam. 2: 1-10; 2 Kings 4: 11-17; Gen. 16: 1-6; Ps. 127: 3; Ex. 1: 15-22; 2: 1-10; 1 Peter 2: 2; Heb. 5: 13)

Bride:

See also Wife, Marriage, and Groom: Covenant relationship; the church or the remnant; unfaithfulness or faithfulness in the natural or the spiritual things; miraculous transformation. (Ephesians 5: 31-32; Hos. 1: 2; 2 Corinthians 6: 14; 11: 2; Rev. 19: 7-9; 20-22; John 21-10; Is. 62: 5)

Brother:

See also Sister and Friend: The Holy Spirit; a spiritual brother in the Church; yourself; someone who has similar qualities to you; the brother himself; can be disorderly, or in need of admonishment, or weak, or evil, in need, or can be falsely judged. (Hebrews 13: 3; 1 Cor. 1: 1; Amos 1; 9; 1 Cor. 8: 11-13; 2 Thess. 3: 6; James: 1: 9; Romans 14: 10-21; 2 Thess. 3: 15; 1 Timothy 5: 1)

Brother-in-law:

See also Sister-in-law: Same as a brother, yet under the law; minister involved in another church; yourself; the brother-in-law himself; adversity; someone who has similar qualities to him. (Esther 7: 6; Exodus 18: 17; Gal. 3: 5, 42-26; 4: 21; Romans 4: 13-15; 1 Timothy 5: 1)

Carpenter:

Jesus, a preacher of the gospel. (2 Kings 22: 6; Is. 41: 7; Mark 6: 3)

Clown:

The carnal nature; playing with God; childishness; work of the flesh. (Eccl. 7: 4)

Daughter:

Child of God; a ministry that is your child in the Spirit; look at similar character traits in yourself; the child herself; prophecy; complacent; dutiful; beautiful; given to lust; ideal. (Ez. 16: 44; Joel 2: 28; Proverbs 31: 29; Gen. 19: 30-38; Judges 11: 36-39; Is. 32: 9-11; Ps. 45: 9-13)q

Doctor:

See also Hospital: Healer; authority; the wisdom of the world; minister; Jesus. (2 Chronicles 16: 12; Mark 2: 17; 5: 26)

Driver:

The one in control of the ministry, marriage, life, etc. What is the of the driver, and whom are they driving? (2 Kings 9: 20)

Drunkard:

Also Drug Addict: Under the influence of a spirit that is either righteous or wrong; controlled; rebellion; completely overcome in an addicted manner to something other than the Lord (like having another god before them); self-indulging; destruction; turbulent seas; lightheadedness; error;

Spiritual Blindness:

Global commotion; persecution; debased mind; poverty; corrupted justice; mind turmoil; unbridled lust; disorderly behavior; slumber. (Acts 2: 13-18; Eph. 5: 18; Luke 21: 34; Rev. 17: 4; Is. 49: 26; 19: 14; 28: 7;

29: 9-11; 5: 22, 23; ; Jer. 25: 15-29; Prov. 20: 1; 23: 21; Ps. 107: 25-27; 1 Thess. 5: 6, 7; Rom. 13: 13)

Employee:

Also Servants: Showing who is in submission in a certain situation; actual person; servant. (Col. 3: 22)

Employer:

Also Master: Showing who is in charge in a certain situation; Good or evil authority depending on the character and actions of the person in a dream; Pastor; Satan. (Col. 4: 1)

Family:

See also Father, Mother, Daughter, and Son: Church family; or natural family; assembly or team or group in covenant together; harmony and oneness; eternal bond; order or disorder; fellowship; relationships. (Eph. 1: 5; 3: 14-15; 5: 23; Gen. 13: 16; Col. 3: 18-21; Matt. 10: 13; Heb. 9: 15; Col. 1: 12; Rev. 22: 3-5; 1 Cor. 11: 3; Rom. 8: 17)

Farmer:

See Barn and Field: Minister in any capacity; Pastor; Preacher; sowing and reaping; diligence; rewards; harvest. (Mark 4: 14; Prov. 24: 30-34; Luke 12: 16-21; 2 Cor. 9: 6-11; Gen. 8: 22; Matt. 13: 30)

Father:

See also Family, Mother, Daughter, and Son: Father God; the Holy Spirit; an authority that is natural and spiritual; birthright; tradition; satan; natural father; supplier of needs; trainer; the one who nourishes; head of household; Father's house can be the Temple of heaven. (John 8: 44, 54; Hos. 11: 1-3; Matt. 7: 8-11; Is. 1: 2; Ex. 6: 14; John 2: 14-16; 14: 2)

Father-in-law:

See also Mother-in-Law: Same as above but a father under the law; the actual father-in-law himself; advisor. (Exodus 18: 17; Gal. 3: 5, 42-26; 4: 21; Romans 4: 13-15)

Foreigner:

Also Sojourner, Stranger, Unknown Man, and Alien: Not of the fold; someone to view with care; not a citizen of heaven (because of not accepting Jesus Christ as Lord); a wanderer; cursed; no longer a part of the world (as living in but not being of). (Gen. 11: 1-9; Lam. 5: 2; Ruth 5: 10; Matt. 8: 20; Eph. 2: 19; 3: 1-6; 1 Cor. 4: 11; 1 Peter 2: 11)

Friend:

See also Brother and Sister: Jesus; faithfulness; can tempt others to sin; sacrifice; similar to the dreamer in position in society, personality traits both in strengths and weaknesses and things that appeal to them. (1 Sam. 15: 8; 18: 1; 20: 11-16; Prov. 17: 17; 18: 24; Ps. 41: 9; Prov. 27: 7; John 15: 13; Du. 13: 6-8)

Giant:

Angel; demon; challenge; the mountain that needs overcoming. (Numbers 13: 32-33; 2 Sam. 21: 16- 22; Gen. 6: 4; Du. 2: 10-11, 21; 9: 2; 1 Chron. 20: 4-8)

Governor:

Kings, Judges, Caesars, Emperors, Princes, Pharaohs, and Rulers: Person in charge in the Church and natural; government, authority; the Lord; rule and reign. (Mal. 1:8; Acts 23: 24, 26; Ps. 84: 3; 100: 4; 2 Chron. 18: 33; 1 Kings 16: 16; Prov. 21: 1)

Grandchild:

Inherited blessing or iniquity; one's spiritual heritage; an actual grandchild; a ministry that came from someone who came out of your ministry; heir; virtue in the family. (Ex. 34: 7; 2 Kings 17: 41; 1 Tim. 5: 4)

Grandmother:

Also Grandfather: Righteous for an unrighteous spiritual inheritance; past; wisdom. (Proverbs 13: 22; 2 Tim. 1: 5).

Groom:

See also Marriage and Bride: Christ the Bridegroom; marriage; headship; God. (John 3: 29; Ez. 16: 8-14)

Guard:

See also Police: Protection and defense; vigilance and sober-mindedness; keep prisoners in prison; power; training of soul and flesh; God's ability to keep us. (2 Tim. 1: 12; Eph. 6: 10-18; 1 Peter 5: 8; 2 Kings 10: 25; Acts 16: 27; Prov. 4: 13; 13: 6; 21: 23)

Guest:

Angel; messenger; celebration; witnesses of God's sovereignty and justice; the Lord Jesus in our hearts; evil presence. (1 Sam. 16: 5; Zeph. 1: 7; Rev. 19: 9; 22: 17; John 14: 6; Gen. 12: 16; 19: 3, 24)

Harlot:

Also Prostitute: Adultery; temptation; snare; covetousness; worldly Church; enticement; unfaithful Israel or Church; loves God much when forgiven. (Rev. 17: 5; Jer. 2: 20-24; 3: 3; Is. 1: 2; Prov. 2: 16;-19 5: 3-5; 6: 26; 7: 6-27;-23 9: 13-18; Hos. 2: 7; 4: 12; Luke 7: 36-50; Matt. 21: 31; 1 Cor. 6: 9-11)

Husband:

Also see Marriage and Groom: The Lord Jesus; satan; actual person; to be honored; ex-husband could be bondage to the world. (Is. 54: 5; Prov. 5: 18, 19; 1 Cor. 14: 34, 35; 1 Peter 3: 7; Gen. 3: 16; Jer. 3: 20)

Judge:

Also Kings, Governors, Caesar's, Emperors, Princes, Pharaohs, and Rulers: Father God; conscienceless toward sin or guilt; authority; satan; one anointed to make decisions; accuser; unjust; Jesus. (1 Cor. 11: 31; Psalm 75: 7; 94: 20; Acts 23: 3; 17: 31; James 5: 9; Mic. 7: 3)

Lawyer:

Also Attorney: Counselor; prosecutor or accuser; defender; Christ; legalism; advocate; mediator. (Rev. 12: 10; Luke 11: 46; 22: 66-71; Titus 3: 13; 1 John 2: 1; 14: 16, 26)

Man (unknown person):

Also see Old Man and Foreigner: God's messenger; demonic messenger; evil motive; if a kind stranger: Jesus; Son of Man; the humanity of Jesus. (Heb. 13: 2; 2: 14-16; John 3: 16; Luke 19: 10; Gen. 11: 1-9; Lam. 5: 2; Ruth 5: 10; Matt. 8: 20; Eph. 2: 19; 3: 1-6; 1 Cor. 4: 11; 1 Peter 2: 11)

Mother:

Church; Jerusalem; charity and love; comfort; Holy Spirit; meddler; mother herself; spiritual mother; teacher; tremendously evil end time apostate church. (Gal. 4: 26; Gen. 3: 20; Ps. 87: 5-6; Rev. 17: 5; Hos. 2: 2, 5; Prov. 31; Rom. 16: 13; Ez. 23: 2; Jer. 50: 12).

Mother-in-law:

Also see Father-in-law: Church; Jerusalem above; meddler; mother-in-law herself; false teachers; tremendously evil end time apostate church. (Gal. 4: 26; Gen. 3: 20; Ps. 87: 5-6; Rev. 17: 5; Hos. 2: 2, 5; Prov. 31; Rom. 16: 13; Ez. 23: 2; Jer. 50: 12)

Old Man:

Carnality; wisdom. (Rom. 6: 6, 5: 17; Heb. 13: 2; 2: 14-16; John 3: 16; Luke 19: 10; Gen. 11: 1-9; Lam. 5: 2; Ruth 5: 10; Matt. 8: 20; Eph. 2:1, 19; 3: 1-6; 1 Cor. 2: 14; 4: 11; 1 Peter 2: 11)

Police:

See also Guard, Lawyer, and Judge: Spiritual authority of the Church; Pastor or Elders; protection; natural authority; angels or demons; enforcer of the law's curse. (Hebrews 1: 7, 14; Luke 12: 11; 22: 25; Ps. 94: 20; 2 Cor. 10: 8; Titus 2: 15; 2 Tim. 1: 12; Eph. 6: 10-18; 1 Peter 5: 8; 2 Kings 10: 25; Acts 16: 27; Prov. 4: 13; 13: 6; 21: 23)

Preacher and Pastor:

Also Priest and Prophet: Representing God; a preacher's wife could be the Church; spiritual authority. (Jer. 3: 15; 23: 1; Jude 24-25; Rom. 10: 14; 12: 1-2; 2 Cor. 11: 13; Heb. 4: 14- 16; Gal. 3: 27)

Sister:

See Brother: Sister in Jesus; similar qualities you see in yourself or someone else; herself; the Church. (Matt. 12: 50; Rom. 14: 10-21; 16: 1; 2 John 13; Hebrews 13: 3; Amos 1; 9; 1 Cor. 1: 1; 8: 11-13; Luke 10: 38-42; 2 Thess. 3: 6, 15; James: 1: 9; 2: 15; 1 Timothy 5: 2)

Sister-in-law:

See also Brother-in-Law: Same as a sister only under the law; Minister involved in another church; yourself; the sister-in-law herself; someone who has similar qualities to her. (Esther 7: 6; 1 Timothy 5: 2; Exodus 18: 17; Gal. 3: 5, 42-26; 4: 21; Romans 4: 13-15)

Soldier:

See also Guard and Police: Spiritual warfare; God's ability to keep us; angel; warring in the Spirit; a demon with the purpose of warring; persecution; working for the Lord. (Rev. 12: 7, 10; 2 Tim. 1: 12; 2: 4; Phil. 2: 25;

Eph. 6: 10-18; 1 Peter 5: 8; 2 Kings 10: 25; Acts 16: 27; Prov. 4: 13; 13: 6; 21: 23)

Son:

See also daughter: Child of God; a ministry that is your child in the Spirit; look at similar character traits in yourself; the child himself; prophesy; complacent; dutiful; characteristics of lust; ideal. (Ez 16: 44; Joel 2: 28; Proverbs 31: 29; Gen. 19: 30-38; Judges 11: 36-39; Is. 32: 9-11; Ps. 45: 9-13)

Teacher:

See also Classroom and School: Jesus Christ; Holy Spirit; the revelation of God; important instruction; a gift from God to the body; can be evil; five-fold ministry; authority. (John 3: 2; Eph. 4: 11; Ps. 18: 34;71: 17; 144: 1; Heb. 8: 11; 1 Tim. 4: 1-3; Job 21: 22; 2 Sam. 22: 35; Prov. 3: 5; Mark 11: 13-17; 2 Kings 2: 15; 5: 22; Phil. 2: 5-11; 1 Cor. 11: 1)

Thief:

Satan; deceiver; loss; works of the flesh; condemned if not repented of; cannot be named among the brethren; Jesus coming like a thief. (1 Cor. 6: 10; Prov. 6: 30; 1 Thess. 5: 2; Rev. 3: 3; 16: 15; Is. 1: 23; John 12: 6; Job 24: 14; John 10: 1-10; Eph. 4: 28)

Wife:

See also Bride and Marriage: Israel; the wife herself; joined together; submission; Bride of Christ; Holy Spirit; covenant relationship; the church or the remnant; unfaithfulness or faithfulness in the natural things or the spiritual things; miraculous **transformation**. (Ephesians 5: 23-32; Hos. 1: 2; 2 Corinthians 6: 14; 11: 2; Rev. 19: 7-9, 20-22; 21: 8; John 21-10; Is. 62: 5; Ez. 16: 8-14; 1 Corinthians 7:33; Gal. 4: 24)

Witch:

Rebellion; slander; non-submissive wife, lust for power and authority; church member or employee; controlling spirit type of Jezebel, both in a male or a female; seduction; worldly Church; forbidden. (1 Samuel 15: 23; 2 Kings 9: 22; 2 Chron. 33: 6; Gal. 3: 1; 5: 20; Du. 18: 9-14; Ex. 22: 18)

Woman (Unknown):

See Man and Harlot: Angel; demon; witchcraft; seducing Spirit; temptation; yourself. (Proverbs 2: 16; 23: 27; Heb. 13: 2; 2: 14-16; John 3: 16; Luke 13: 21; 9: 10;

Personal Reflection

1) Who are the people you have ever met in your dream now that you have the Interpretation?

_____

_____

_____

_____

_____

_____

2) If the Interpretation of any of the people you have seen in the past is bad, go ahead and pray against the evil effect of that dream.

_____

_____

_____

_____

_____

_____

Chapter 10

Dream Interpretation Numbers

One:

Also First: New; beginning; unity; timing; position or order primacy; deity; sufficiency. (Du. 6:4; John 17: 21; Matt. 6: 33; Ex. 20: 3; Rev. 1: 11, 17; 2: 8; Is. 44: 6; 45: 5-6)

Two:

Witnessing; separation; discernment; wholeness in marriage; division; enmity; opposition; dividing light and darkness; the relationship between God and man is closely tied to our relationship with a man. (Gen. 1: 6-8, 27; 2: 24; 16: 21; Ex. 31: 18; Ecc. 4: 9-10; Matt. 19: 5-6; 22: 37-40; 1 Tim. 5: 19; John 8: 17; Rev. 11: 2-4)

Third:

Complete; perfection; witness; divine fullness; solid attributes; Godhead; conform; resurrection power over sin; divine fullness. (Romans 3: 9; 6: 9; 1 Sam. 3: 8; Jonah 1: 16-17; 20: 1-9; 1 John 5: 6-7; Col. 2: 9; Eph. 3: 19; 4: 13; John 1: 16)

Four:

World; earth; creation; creative work; four winds; four seasons; four corners of the earth; rule and reign over the earth; global implications such as east, west, north, south; territorial specific realm implications. (Gen. 2: 10; 41: 34; Rev. 5: 9; 7: 1, 9; 13: 7; Is. 58: 6-10; Ez. 42: 20; 46: 21; Lev. 11: 20-27; 27: 31; John 8: 34; 1 Cor. 15: 39)

Five:

Grace; atonement; fivefold ministry; service (five fingers on the hand); bondage; complete wellness. (Is. 1: 12-14; Matt. 25: 2; Eph. 4: 11; Mark 6: 38-40; Luke 9: 13-16; Gen. 1: 20-23)

Six:

Man; beast; Satan; flesh; carnal; toil and strain of the flesh or natural realm; work; sorrow; secular completeness. (Rev. 13: 18; 1 Sam. 17: 4-7; Gen. 1: 26-31; 4: 17-18; 2 Peter 3: 8; 2 Sam. 21: 20; Num. 35: 15)

Seven:

Completion; finished work; perfection; rest; perfection in the Spirit. (Gen. 2: 1-3; Lev. 14: 7; 16: 14, 19; Matt. 18: 21-22; Jude 14; Rev. 2: 1; 8: 2; 12: 3)

Eight:

Circumcision of the flesh; liberty; salvation; a new beginning; resurrection life; die to self. (Gen. 17: 12; 1 Peter 3: 20-21; 2 Chron. 29: 17; 2 Peter 1: 14)

Nine:

Fruit of the Spirit; gifts of the Spirit; finality; harvest; the fullness of development. (Matt. 27: 45; Judges 4: 1-3; Gal. 5: 22-23; 1 Cor. 12: 4-11)

Ten:

Government; law (commandments); order; tithe; measure; trial; testing. (Lev. 27: 32; Ex. 34: 28; Rev. 2: 10; 12: 3; Matt. 25:1-13)

Eleven:

End; finish; final; incomplete; disorder; lawlessness. (Gen. 27: 9; 32: 33; Du. 11: 8; Ex. 26: 7; Matt. 20: 9-12)

Twelve:

Divine government and election; apostolic fullness; discipleship; The Church; people of God; united; oversight. (Gen. 49: 28; Numbers 13: 1-16; Matt. 3: 14; Luke 9: 1-2; 22: 30; Rev. 12: 1; 21: 12; Rev. 22: 2; Ex. 15: 27; 29: 15; 1 Cor. 1: 10) we

Thirteen:

Rebellion; rejection; backsliding. (Gen. 14: 4; Esther 9: 11; 1 King 7: 1)

Fourteen:

Passover; recreate, reproduce; servant. (Ex. 12: 6; 1 Kings 8: 65; Num. 9: 5; Gen. 31:

Fifteen:

Deliverance; grace; freedom; rest. (Lev. 23: 6-7; Hos. 3: 2; Gen. 7: 20; 2 Kings 20: 6

Sixteen:

Not under the law because of love; free; salvation. (Acts 27: 34; 37-38)

Fifteen:

Deliverance; grace; freedom; rest. (Lev. 23: 6-7; Hos. 3: 2; Gen. 7: 20; 2 Kings 20:6)

Sixteen:

Not under the law because of love; free; salvation. (Acts 27: 34; 37-38)

Seventeen:

Spiritual order; incomplete; immature. (Gen. 37: 2; 1 Chron. 25: 5; Jer. 32: 9)

Eighteen:

Bondage, judgment; destruction; captivity. (Judges 10: 7-8; Luke 13: 11-16)

Nineteen:

Faith; void of self-righteousness; ashamed; barren of flesh or Spirit; repentance. (2 Samuel 2: 30; Rom. 6: 21)

Twenty:

Holy; redemption. (Ex. 30: 12-14; Rev. 4: 4)

Twenty-one:

Victory

Twenty-four:

Perfection in government; priesthood; consecration; maturity. (Rev. 4: 4-10; Josh. 4: 2-9; 1 Chron. 24: 3-5; 25: 1-12; 1 Kings 19: 19)

Thirty:

Beginning of ministry; maturity for the church; the blood of Christ. (Luke 3: 23; Gen. 41: 16; Num. 4: 3)

Forty:

Trials; testing. (Matt. 4: 2; Num. 13: 25; 14: 33-34; Ex. 34:27-28; Matt. 26: 15; Acts 1: 6; 7: 30) Fifty: Pentecost; Holy Spirit; jubilee; liberty; freedom.Coming out of the wilderness(Lev. 23: 16; 25: 10-11; Ex. 26: 5-6; 2 Kings 2: 7;
Num. 8: 21)

Seventy:

Transference of God's Spirit; multitude; increase; restoration. (Num. 11: 16-29; Gen. 4: 24; 11: 26; 46: 27; Ex. 1: 5-6; 15: 27; 24: 1-9; Luke 10: 1)

Seventy-five:

Cleansing and purifying; separating. (Gen. 12: 4; Dan. 12: 5-13) One hundred: Fullness; people of promise. (Mark 5: 20; 10: 30; Gen. 26: 12)

One hundred and Twenty:

Start of life in the Spirit; end of flesh life. (Acts 1: 5; 2 Chron. 3: 4; 5: 12; Gen. 6: 3; Du. 34: 7)

One hundred and forty-four:

God's fullness in all He has created. (Rev. 7: 1-6; 14: 1-3; 21: 17; 1 Chron. 25: 7)

One hundred and Fifty:

End of the judgment by water. (Gen. 8: 3)

One hundred and Fifty-three:

Bringing in the harvest; revival. (John 21: 6-4)

Two Hundred:

Inadequacy of needs being met in the natural and Spirit. (2 Sam. 14: 26; Josh. 7: 21; John 6: 7; Gen. 11: 19)

Three hundred:

God's chosen; God's remnant. (Judges 7 & 8; 15: 4; Gen. 5: 22; 6: 15)

Three hundred ninety:

God's chosen; God's remnant as in the nation of Israel. (Is. 7: 8; Ez. 4: 5)

Six-Six-Six:

Antichrist; Satan; the number of a man; the beast's mark. (Rev. 13: 18; Dan. 3: 17)

Thousands:

Coming to maturity. (Joshua 3: 3-4; 1 Sam. 17: 5, 33; Eph. 4: 13; Rev. 12: 18; 14: 9-11)

Two Thousand:

Church age ending in the resurrection. (Joshua 3: 4)

Ten Thousand:

God's army was taught and led by God. (Du. 33: 2-3, Jude 14)

Twelve Thousand:

The Lord's mighty army. (Rev. 7: 5-8)

One hundred and forty-four thousand:

The salvation of the world. (Rev. 7: 4)

Personal Reflection

1) What numbers have you always seen in your dream?

_____

_____

_____

_____

_____

_____

_____

2) If it is good, anoint yourself and say, I stand in agreement with the will of God for my life and everything that concerns me. I activate these numbers in my life by the blood of Jesus Christ. May I begin to enjoy the promises of God for me in It?

_____

_____

_____

_____

_____

_____

_____

3) If it is bad, anoint yourself and say I deactivate the evil effect of these numbers in my life and everything that concerns me. by this anointing, I break the yoke of the numbers, and I set myself free from the powers backing it up, and I command it to be consumed in Jesus name.

_____

_____

_____

_____

_____

_____

_____

_____

_____

Chapter 11

Dream Interpretation for Animals

1)   Alligator:

See Leviathan, Also Crocodile and Dinosaur: Bending; crooked; meandering; snake; monster; devious; distorted; ancient demon; large, evil creature that cannot be tamed with the natural strength of man; principality; evil spirit; ancient demonic control; only the Lord has power over; dragon. (Is. 27: 1; 51: 9; Job 7: 12; 26: 12-13; 41: 1-10; Ps. 74: 14; 104: 26; Rev. 6: 7; 9: 1-19; 13: 1-18).

2) Ant:

Hardworking: ability to prepare; wisdom. (Prov. 6: 6-8; 30:25).

3) Bat:

Night dweller; thought of to suck blood; unclean; flying creature often related to witchcraft.

4) Vampires:

Satanic torment (Deut. 14: 18; Is. 2: 19-21; Lev. 11: 19).

5) Bear:

Evil men; danger (if one plays dead, a bear will not pursue them, so be crucified and die daily); Russia; wicked ruler over poor people, vindictiveness that is severe; antichrist of the last days; end time dominion and rule; financial matters as in: bear market; demonic force, hungry for something you have (2 Sam. 17: 8; Dan. 7: 5; Is. 11: 7; Rev. 13: 2; Amos 5: 19; 2 Kings 2: 23-24; Prov. 17: 12).

6)   Bees:

Busy bodies; gossip; group of people; can produce sweet honey, or sting and wound; enemies that crowd around us; higher demonic power but less lethal (1 Tim. 5: 13; Judges 14: 8; Du. 1: 44; Psalms 118: 12).

7)   Bird:

Holy Spirit; evil spirits; wicked rulers; nations that are hostile; Kingdom of God; a mother's love; God's provision. (Matt. 6: 29; 13: 32; 23: 37; Is. 46: 11).

8)   Black Panther:

Higher level witchcraft.

9)   Crane:

Alone. (Is. 38: 14; Hos. 7: 11).

10) Camel:

A servant's heart; to bear the load. (Gen. 24: 10, 31-32).

11) Cat:

Also Tigers, Leopards and Cheetahs: Unclean spirit; danger lying in wait; crafty; mysterious, strong self-will; witchcraft; someone that is unattainable; unless personal pet. In the case of a personal pet, a cat can mean something or someone dear to your heart. A personal pet that is a leopard; could be a pet sin; a watching demonic spirit, independent thinker (Jer. 5:6, 13: 23; Hos. 13: 7).

12) Cheetahs:

Also Tigers, Leopards and Cats: Eaters of flesh and drinkers of blood.

13) Chicken:

Also Hen, Rooster, and Chick: A gatherer; to mother; Israel. (Luke 13: 34; 22: 34; Matt. 23: 27; John 18: 27).

14) Cobra:

Spirit of control and manipulation.

15) Cow:

Also Heifer, Bull with big horns or cow with a big horn ,Calf and Cattle: The young: believers who are sanctified; agile; sacrifice; food; playful; worship of golden calves: immorality; great sin; punishment; an apostasy; blood of is not sufficient; evil men; mighty men; God's sacrifice and strength; ashes of sacrifice kept, mixed with water to purify; slaughtered and burned outside the camp; for sacrifice must be without blemish and never been in bondage to sin (never yoked); fall short of the sacrifice of Christ; expediency that is not proper; festive joy with shame; slow laborious change(Num. 18: 17; 19: 1-22; Lev. 9: 2-3; Amos 6: 4; Ps. 22: 13; 29: 6; 68: 30; Ex. 32: 4-6, 21-35; 1 Cor. 10: 6-8; Matt. 10: 29-30; Luke 15: 23, 27; Heb. 9: 13; 10: 4; Du. 33: 17; Is. 34: 6-7; Gen. 15: 9; Judges 14: 18; Jer. 50: 11).

16) Crab:

Hard shell, not easy to approach.

17) Crocodile:

See Leviathan, Dinosaur and Alligator: Bending; crooked; meandering; snake; monster; devious; distorted; ancient demon; large, evil creature that cannot be tamed with the natural strength of man; principality; evil spirit; ancient demonic control; only the Lord has power over; dragon; big mouth, something that can drag you down, vicious verbal attack (Is. 27: 1; 51: 9; Job 7: 12; 26: 12-13; 41: 1-10; Ps. 74: 14; 104: 26; Rev. 6: 7; 9: 1-19; 13: 1-18)

18) Deer:

Also Hind: Seeking water; ability to leap; quickness in stride; comeliness; our soul longing for the Lord. (Is. 35: 6; Ps. 18: 32; 42: 1-2; Song 2: 17; 2 Sam. 22: 34).

19) Dinosaur:

See Leviathan, Dinosaur and Alligator: A high level of demonic attack; spiritual wickedness in high places; antichrist; Satan. (Rev. 12:3-9; 13: 2-4; 16: 1; 20: 2)

20) Dog:

Note type of dog and relationship to dog: biting dog is dissension; hypocrite; attack against God's work; accusation; if a personal pet: something or someone dear to your heart; personal pet that is a wolf: pet sin, or warning you of an attack on the sheep; Judases; watchman as in Elder or prophet as watchdog; returning to sin; false teachers. (Prov. 26: 11-17; Phil. 3:2; Ez. 3: 17; Gal. 5 15; Ps. 22: 16; Rev. 22: 15; 2 Peter 2: 22; Matt. 7: 6)

21) Donkey:

Also Mule: Hard headed; endurance; self-willed, single-minded, determined, and unyielding; riding: victory over self-will and humility; stubborn (Ex. 4: 20; Mark 11: 2; Prov. 26: 3; Num. 22: 25; 2 Peter 2: 16; Hosea 8: 9)

22) Dragon:

See Leviathan, Dinosaur and Alligator: A high level of demonic attack; spiritual wickedness in high places; antichrist; Satan. (Rev. 12:3-9; 13: 2-4; 16: 1; 20: 2)

23) Dove:

The Holy Spirit; peace and new life; a sin offering; burnt offering; cleansing; mercy. (Gen. 8: 8-12; Matt. 3: 16; 10: 16; Lev. 5: 7-14, 14: 21-22; John 1: 32)

24) Duck:

False or quack as in a charlatan (Jeremiah 5:31; Matthew 7:15).

25) Eagle:

Soaring in the Spirit; good or evil leader; strength, power, and swiftness in both judgment and in delivering God's people from trouble; the United States of America; Prophet of God. (Isaiah 40: 31, 46: 11; Jer. 48: 40, Ez. 17: 3, 7; Ex. 19: 4; Rev. 12: 14)

26) Feathers:

Protection; shield; provision of ability to fly and sore. (Ez. 17: 3-7; Ps. 91: 4; Dan. 4: 33) Fowler: To mesmerize; to be trapped. (Ps. 91: 4)

27) Fish:

The newly saved; men's souls; clean and unclean men or spirits; miraculous provision of food in mass. (Ez. 4: 19; Lev. 11: 9-12; Matt 4: 19; 17: 24)

28) Flea:

Not substantial; annoyance; subtle; inconvenience. (1 Sam. 24: 14)

29) Fly:

Beelzebub; Demons; corruption of the house or possession by demonic spirits of the person. (Ecc.10: 1; Matt. 12: 24)

30) Fox:

Also Jackal: Secret sins; crafty man; enemies of the cross; skill for evil; desolation and crying in the night; divining prophets; suck the life flow from lambs (blood). (Jer. 9: 11; Rev. 13: 11; Is. 35: 6-7; Ez. 13: 4-6; Song 2: 15; Luke 13: 32)

31) Frog:

Demon spirits; lying nature; sorcery; speaking curses; counterfeit of conscience, lust, sexual spirit (Rev. 16: 13; Ex. 8: 1-15; Ps. 78: 45)

32) Grasshopper:

Also Locust: Trouble and devastation to crops; instrument of God's judgment upon nations that are rebellious; destroyer; subordinate position; numbers of a mighty army; encumbering task; trivial. (Ex. 10: 1-20; Rev. 9: 7-11; Is. 40: 22; Num. 13: 33; Joel 2: 1-11, 25; Lev. 11: 20-23; Mark 1: 6; Eccl. 12: 5)

33) Goat:

Carnal, fleshly Christians; unbelief; Christian or group of Christians walking in sin; the cursed, scapegoat or goat of removal showing that our sins have been removed as far as the east is from the west; opposite of lambs; carriers of sin; our need to obtain forgiveness of sin; mixed with sheep, but not called the shepherds own. (Ex. 25: 4; Matt. 25: 31-46; Lev. 16: 8, 15, 20-22; Ps. 103: 12; Heb. 13: 12).

34) Hare:

See Rabbit.

35) Hamster:

Running around in circles

36) Hippopotamus:

Big mouth, bossy spirit, great influencer

37) Hornet:

Higher demonic power, less lethal; or God sending something ahead to clear a path (Exodus 23:28)

38) Horse:

Instruments of battle; power and strength of the flesh; time period of work; a powerful work of God on the earth, in the Spirit; tenaciousness, single-mindedness and aggressiveness; in transportation: battle; not to trust in over the name of the Lord. (This would carry over into our modern day weapons and modes of transport.) (Job 39: 19; Ps. 32: 9; 33: 17; 66: 12; Prov. 26: 3; Jer. 5: 8; 8: 6; Rev. 6: 1-8; 19: 11, 14, 19, 21; Zech. 1: 8; 10: 3; 2 Kings 2: 11; Hos. 14: 3; James 3: 3; Amos 8: 11; John 16: 2)

Different color horses are important:

- **Black:**

Famine; evil.
Bay (flame-colored): Anointing, power, fire.
Pale: Death.

- **Red:**

Persecution, bloodshed; enemy warring against God's people. White: War of conquest; God's mighty army)

39) Lamb:

Also Sheep: Jesus as our sacrifice; true believers; gentleness; blamelessness and purity led to the slaughter; saints; the church; Israel. (Is. 53: 7; 2 Sam. 2: 17; Luke 10: 3; Matt. 10: 6; 25: 33; John 1: 29, 36; 1 Peter 1: 19)

40) Leopards:

See also Tigers, Cheetahs and Cats. Leviathan, Crocodile and Dinosaur: Creature that cannot be tamed with the natural strength of man; demon; evil spirit; ancient demonic control; only the Lord has power over. (Job 41: 1-10; Ps. 74: 14; 104: 26)

41) Leviathan:

See also Crocodile, Alligator, Dragon and Dinosaur: Bending; crooked; meandering; snake; monster; devious; distorted; ancient demon; large, evil creature that cannot be tamed with the natural strength of man; principality; evil spirit; ancient demonic control; only the Lord has power over; dragon. (Is. 27: 1; 51: 9; Job 7: 12; 26: 12-13; 41: 1-10; Ps. 74: 14; 104: 26; Rev. 6: 7; 9: 1-19; 13: 1-18)

42) Lice:

Accusation; shame; plague. (Ex. 8: 16-18)

43) Lion:

Jesus; conqueror; overcoming bold saints; Satan the devourer; warrior; transformation; victory; persecution; dominions of the world; antichrist.leader, religious leader (Ez. 1: 10; Prov. 28: 1;30: 30; Is. 11: 6-8; John 18: 37; Rev. 5: 5; 13: 2; 17: 14; 19: 16; 1 Peter 5: 8; Ps. 22: 13; 91: 13; Dan. 7: 1-4)

44) Lizard:

unclean; lying (long "tale") (Leviticus 11:29-31)

45) Locusts:

See Grasshopper. Pig: Also Sow and Swine: An unclean (fleshly) people; legalistic Christians; dull minded to spiritual things; phony and hypocritical; a foolish woman; false teachers; detestable things. (Matt. 7: 6; Prov. 11: 22; Is. 65: 4; 66: 3; 2 Peter 2: 22; Ps. 80: 13)

46) Owl:

Also Lilith, Screech Owls and Night Hags: Wisdom through earthly means or from above; evil spirit; unclean spirit; night creature; routinely secluded. Monitoring spirit: territorial witchcraft power (Is. 13: 21; 34: 13-14; 43: 20; Ps. 102: 6; Job 30: 29)

47) Panther (black):

high level of witchcraft (see cat and Lion)

48) Rabbit: Also Hare: Satan; evil spirits; pagan celebration of Easter; rapid multiplication; sexual torment
(Deut. 14: 7; Lev. 11:6; Josh. 19: 20)

49) Raven: See buzzard. Sparrow: Provision; food; God's care for his creation. (Matt. 10: 29-30) Wings: Refuge; God's presence; safety; ability to fly away and escape danger. (Ps. 91: 4, 17: 8, 61: 4)

50) Scorpion: Evil spirits; sin nature; burdens that are heavy; lust of the flesh; deception; a stringing deadly pain; satanic; spirit of the antichrist; poisonous; someone wanting to do you in, witchcraft. (Luke 10: 19; Rev. 9: 3, 5, 10; 1 Cor. 15: 56; Rom. 7: 23; 1 Kings 12: 11; Du. 8: 15; 2 Chron. 10: 11)

51) Serpent: Also Snake: Satan; earthly, sensual wisdom; crafty and cunning; Christ made sin for us; cursed; criticism and gossip, persecution if viper; divination if python or constrictor; beguiling; drunkenness; malice; evil that is sudden; enemies; vileness of hate of the sinner. (Gen. 3: 1; 49: 17; Rev. 12: 9; 20: 2; 20: 2; Mark 3: 7; Acts 16: 16; Matt. 10: 16;

John 3: 14; Prov. 23: 31-32; Ps. 58: 3-4; Eccl. 10: 8; Is. 14: 29)

52) Sheep: See Lamb. Snake: See Serpent. Spider: False doctrine; unstable; without any deity; enticing demonic presence. (Is. 59: 5; Eccl. 7: 26; Job 8: 14; Prov. 8: 14; 27: 18; 30: 24)

53) Snake: backbiting, divination, false accusations, false prophecies, gossip, long tales, slander (Numbers 21:6; Matthew 23:33; Luke 10:19)

54) Tigers: Also Cheetah, Leopards and Cats.

55) Wolf: Plan to destroy God's flock; deviant; wolf in sheep's clothing; brazen; false prophet; opportunistic; prowl round at night. (Matt. 7: 15; 10: 16; John 10: 12; Is. 11: 6; Jer. 5: 6)

56) Worm: Also Maggot: Detested: disease; humility; no dignity; filthiness of the flesh; destruction; eat off of flesh; destructive to vines and tree; likened to the misery and suffering of the lost soul in hell; crucified Messiah. (Ex. 16: 20; Du 28: 39; Is 14: 11, 66: 24, 51: 8; Job 25: 6; Ps. 22: 6; Mark 9

Chapter 12

Dream Interpretation for Metals

- **Brass**:

Judgment of sin; hardness of heart; Word of God; strength; Christ's glory; willful disobedience; judged; man's word; replacement. (Ex. 26: 19; Num. 21: 9; Rev. 1: 15; Is. 48: 4; Heb. 13: 10-13; Ex. 27: 13; 1 Corinthians; 13: 1; 2 Chron. 12: 10)

- **Gold**:

The riches of the glory of God; enduring capacity of the believer as an overcomer; unchanging holiness; wisdom; glory; righteousness; glorifying self when used as adornment or idol worship. (Lam. 4: 2; Ps. 19: 10, 119: 72; Rev. 3: 18, 21: 18. 21; 1 Cor. 3: 12; Ex. 20: 23; Is. 40: 19; Job 22: 25)

- **Iron**:

Also Steel: Power; strongholds; stubborn; strength; blight; strict rules; crushing power; judgment. (Rev. 2: 27; Du. 28: 23; 48; Dan. 2: 40)

- **Lead:**

Heaviness; burden; sinfulness. (Zech. 5: 8; Ex. 15: 10)

- **Silver**:

Understanding; knowledge; purity; cleanliness; redemption; idolatry; Words of God; promises of God; worldly knowledge; cleansed and ready for use; very precious to God; used as a betrayal; the furnace of adversity. (Proverbs 2: 3-4; Ex. 26: 19; Gen. 37: 28; Judges 17: 4; 1 Kings 7: 51; Ez. 7: 19-20; Matt. 26: 15; Is. 1: 22; Acts 19: 24; 1 Cor. 3: 12; Job 28: 1; Ps. 12: 6)

- **Tin**:

Cheap; flimsy; imitation; dross. (Is. 1: 25; 51: 17-22; Ez. 22: 18-19; Ps. 75: 8; 119: 119)

Chapter 13

Dream interpretation for Places

- **Airpcort**:

The church; family; preparation; preparing to fly in the Spirit; delay; tarry; change; power over demonic forces; provision of nourishment, both natural or spiritual; image of approaching terror. (1 Kings 9: 26-28; Ez. 30: 9; Acts 27: 1-2; Ps. 48: 7; Matt. 8: 23-27; 24: 38; 1 Peter 3: 20; Luke 5: 4; Psalms 74: 13-14; Prov. 31: 14; Jer. 23: 22).

- **Bank**:

Reward reserved in heaven; the church; storage; safe; safeguarded; security; protected; money changers in temple driven out. (John 2: 15; Matt. 6: 20; 25: 27; 21: 12; Luke 19: 23).

- **Banquet**:

See also Food, Cafeteria, and Restaurant: Having plenty and being well satisfied with needs; affluence and luxury; abundance; joy and blessings; not regarding the Lord by partying; church; service; a systematic serving of the Word of God; choosing what you want as opposed to receiving what you need; honoring guest; worship; celebrating victory. (Matt 25: 35; 32: 4; Psalm 19: 9-10; John 6: 27, 48-63; 4: 32, 34; 1 Cor. 3: 1-2; Heb. 5: 14; Ester 1: 3-12; 1 Sam. 25: 11, 36; Jer. 51: 34-44; Prov. 9: 13-18; Is. 5: 11-12).

- **Barbershop**:

See also Hair: Changing customs, habits and traditions, the covenant of sins, religiousness; turning from wrong beliefs and strong opinions; the church as a place of vanity or repentance. (1 Cor. 11: 14; Lev. 19: 27; 2 Sam. 14; 25, 26; Judges 16: 17, 22; Is. 3: 17, 24; Song 5: 2, 11).

- **Barn**:

Church; provision; a place to store wealth; deliverance; workplace; security; plenty. (Du. 28: 8; Luke 12: 18, 24; Prov. 3: 10; Matt. 3: 12; 13: 30).

- **Beauty Shop**:

See Hair, Barber Shop, and Women: Preparation; vanity; holiness. (Pro. 31: 30; Hos. 10:5; Ps. 29: 2; 1 Cor. 11:15).

- **Church**:

service; a systematic serving of the Word of God; choosing what you want as opposed to receiving what you need; honoring guests; worship; celebrating victory. (Matt 25: 35; 32: 4; Psalm 19: 9-10; John 6: 27, 48-63; 4: 32, 34; 1 Sam. 25: 11; Jer. 51: 34-44)

- **Building**:

Also Church Building: The church itself; congregation; an essential service; life choices; edification; new body after the resurrection. (Matt. 16: 18; 7: 24-27; Luke 12: 13-21; 1 Tim. 3: 15; Eph. 2: 20; 4: 12; Romans 15: 2; 2 Cor. 5: 1; Hebrews 3: 4)

- **City**:

Characteristics of what the city in the dream is known for; the church; the nature and virtue or lack of in a person; New Jerusalem, the City of our God; apostate church. (Jude 1: 7; Acts 20: 23;; Rev. 18: 10; 21: 18).

- **Classroom**:

See Teacher and School: Small group ministry within the church; God's call of one chosen for learning and teaching; training; center of learning; five-fold ministry. (Job 21: 22; Luke 8: 35; Psalm 143: 10; 18:34; Acts 19: 9; Eph. 4: 11)

- **Countryside**:

See Nation: A quiet time; space to think; peace and tranquility. (Mark 6: 31; 1 Kings 9: 7; 17: 1-7; 19: 9-13; 1 Sam. 22: 5; Ps. 104: 10-18; Gen. 24: 63).

- **Courthouse**:

See also Judge: Time of trial; balance of mercy and judgment; persecution; judgment. (1 Cor. 6: 1; Is. 43: 12; Ps. 94: 20; Du. 17: 6-13).

- **Factory**:

Smooth service to God and organized or the opposite, the church working properly; unorganized; fervor in service. (Luke 2: 49; Rom. 12: 11; Prov. 31: 13; 1 Thess. 2: 9; Acts 20: 35).

- **Garden**:

See also Yard: Increase; work; ministry; church; pleasant; fruitfulness; prospering; pastime; field of labor. (Gen. 2: 8-10; 4: 2-3; Is. 51: 3; 58: 11; Jer. 2: 21; 1 Tim. 4: 14-15).

- **Hospital**:

Also Healing: Ministry of healing; a place to caring; love; wounded church in need of healing; place of the healing because of hearing the Gospel; or learning of Christ God's Son; extended to the brokenhearted; healing as a result of repentance; turning from backsliding; because of faithfulness; healing from spiritual sickness or there because of it; healing from being obedient and following God's will. (Ez. 47: 8- 11; Is. 53: 5; 19: 22-25; 6: 10).

- **Hotel**:

Temporary; migratory; a socially acceptable place to gather; changing church. (Luke 10: 3-31, 33-34).

- **House**:

See also Sanctuary, Temple, Tent or Tabernacle: Also Home: The church; or one's own home; person or family; dwelling place; Tabernacle or Temple of God; the true church; heaven; security or insecurity depending on a dream; center of the family or family of God; people in the church are the household of God; our present life and its condition; a place to relax and be entertained with ungodly things; people in the church are the members of His household; resting place; a place to return to; eternal home or heaven; reference to one's character or reputation; a place where evil demonic spirits dwell; the human body or body as an earthly tent; our body as a place for God and His Spirit to live. (Luke 11: 24; 15: 6; 2 Sam. 14: 13-24; Ruth 1: 21; 4: 3; Acts 16: 31, 34; Heb. 3: 6; 3: 10-21; 1 Chron. 17: 5; Judges 11: 34; 19: 9; Acts 16: 34; Gen. 14: 14; 8: 9; 2 Cor. 5: 6; Eph. 2: 19; 3: 17; Eccl. 12: 5; **DIFFERENT ROOMS AND LOCATIONS**:

- **Attic**:

See also Upstairs, Roof and Two Story: Of the Spirit; the mind; thought; right and wrong attitudes; stored memories; learning; Spirit realm; upper room; history issues, storing things God has given you that get dusty (Acts 1: 12; 2: 1-4).

- **Basement**:

Storage place; flooding; hidden; forgotten; carnal nature; foul; lust; depression; secret sin; hidden or unseen (Jer. 38: 6).

- **Bathroom**:

Repentance; confession; desire; cleansing; removing; expelling. (Lev. 8: 5-6; 14: 8-9; Ps. 51: 1-2; 7-10; Rev. 21: 26-27).

- **Bedroom**:

Rest; privacy; peace; good covenants and wrong covenants; intimacy; slumbering; laziness. (Ps. 4: 4; 139: 8; Is. 28: 18-20; Heb. 18: 4).

- **Childhood home**:

Something from the past that is influencing you today for good or evil; same for a church; family; etc. (1 Timothy 5: 4).

- **Den**:

Relaxed fellowship; too relaxed; notice where the focus is. (Mark 2: 4-5).

- **Dining Room:**

See also Eating: The table of the Lord; communion with the Lord or the brethren; feeding on the Word. (Ho. 7: 6; Heb. 4: 12; 1 Corinthians 11: 24).

- **Dirty and neglected**:

Church or home in need of attention. (Matt. 25: 25-28; Heb. 10: 22; 2 Cor. 7: 1).

- **Garage**:

Protection, storage, ministry potential for outreach. (Du. 28: 8; Luke 12: 18; Matt. 13: 30).

- **Kitchen**:

See also Cafeteria and Restaurant: Preparation for teaching or preaching; the heart of the matter; hunger for the Word; motives; revealing. (Ho. 7: 6; Heb. 4: 12; 1 Corinthians 11: 24).

- **Living Room:**

See also Den: Formal fellowship of church, family, or friends. (Mark 2: 4-5).

- **New**:

New birth; change for the better or worse according to the home's condition; fresh move of the Spirit; revival. (2 Corinthians 5: 17; 2 Cor. 5: 1).

- **Old**:

Older man or ways; past; spiritual inheritance; religious traditions; natural inheritance. (Gen. 12: 1; Jer. 6: 16; Heb. 2: 3).

- **Porch**:

See also Yard: Outreach and evangelism to the church; public place, exhibited; displayed; exposed. (Mark 14: 68; Acts 5: 12; Joel 2: 17).

- **Roof**:

See also Upstairs and Attic: The mind; meditation; logic or natural; shield or covering of protection; heavenly revelation; prayer; declaration; complete overview; ability to see all, both good and evil. (Acts 10: 9; Matt. 10: 27; Luke 12: 3; 2 Sam. 11: 2; Is. 30: 1).

- **Two-story:**

See also Upstairs, Two Story and Attic: Multilevel situation; Spirit and flesh of a person, church, or ministry. (Acts 1: 13-14; 20: 7-8)

- **Upstairs**:

See also Roof, Two-Story, and Attic: Going higher in the Spirit; something that is of the Spirit; Upper room; Pentecost; thought, good or bad; prayer; Spiritual service. (Acts 1: 13-14; 20: 7-8).

- **Work Area:**

Service under development in the Spirit; or of God; work of the flesh. (Gen. 2: 15; Ps. 104: 23; Gal. 2: 16; Eph. 5: 11; John 6: 29; Phil. 3: 2; 1 Cor. 3: 9).

- **Yard:**

See also Garden and Porch: Public part of personal life; in the back could be an event that is behind or over or hidden. (2 Sam. 17: 18; Esther 1: 5; 1 Kings 6: 36; Ex. 27: 9).

- **Library:**

Exploration into knowledge; knowledge stored up; schooling; abundance of the Word; earthly, sensual wisdom. (2 Tim. 2: 15; James 3: 13-18; 1 Cor. 8: 1; Rom. 2: 20; Col. 1: 9).

- **Nation:**

See also Country: Nation may represent actual nation; known characteristics of the nation. (Mark 6: 31; 1 Kings 9: 7; 17: 1-7; 19: 9-13; 1 Sam. 22: 5; Ps. 104: 10-18; Gen. 24: 63).

- **Park**:

See also Garden and Yard: Worship; enjoying God; playful; garden experience (Adam fell, Jesus faced the cross); rest; tranquility; transient's home. (Gen. 2: 8-10; 4: 2-3; Is. 51: 3; 58: 11; Jer. 2: 21; 1 Tim. 4:14-15)

- **Pit**:

Hell; sepulcher; tomb; entrapment; enticement; self-ruination. (Jer. 18: 20; Is. 14: 15; 24: 22; 38: 17- 18; Rev. 9: 1-2; 20: 1-3).

- **Prison**:

Lost souls; Christian held captive by the enemy; rebellion; lawlessness; bondage; persecuted saints; slavery; Sheol or Hades; imprisoned unjustly; release from prison is God's blessing; confinement of personal circumstances; a spiritual condition that is fallen; death; in need of recognition to God. (Gen. 39: 20; Jer. 37: 18; Ps. 68: 6; 142: 7; Gal. 3 22); Rev. 1: 18, 24; Matt. 5: 25-26; 2 Peter 2: 4).\

- **Restaurant**:

See also Cafeteria and Kitchen: Place of ministry; the atmosphere is important; church with good or bad teaching and serving ministry of the Word; gluttony. (Psalm 19: 9-10; John 6: 27; 48-63; 4: 32, 34; Matt 25: 35; 32: 4; 1 Cor. 3: 1-2; Heb. 5: 14).

- **School**:

See Classroom: Church; place of teaching and discipleship; people or work; training; teaching ministry(Job 21: 22; Luke 8: 35; Psalm 143: 10; 18 :34; Acts 19: 9; Is. 28: 10; Matt. 21: 23; Mark 1: 21; Eph. 4: 11).

- **School**:

Elementary: Beginning level of walk with God; milk. (1 Cor. 3: 1-3).

- **Middle or Junior High:**

Level of maturity of a person or teaching being given or received; or of one's walk. (1 Cor. 14: 20).

- **High School:**

Promotion in the dreamer's level to a higher level or could be of teaching being received or given. (1 Cor. 2: 6).

- **College**:

The highest level of learning; promotion in the Spirit; strong meat. (Rom. 15: 21).

- **Shopping Center:**

Also Marketplace: Too much to choose from; churches within the church; view of spiritual, soulish and political atmosphere that is in a church or a community or nation or even in your heart; not to be in the temple of God or present during worship; leaders there to show off how grand they are; can be dishonest gain; wisdom calls out to the people there. (Prov. 7: 12; 2 Kings 7: 1, 8; Ps. 55: 11; Gen. 34: 10, 21; Amos 8: 5; Neh. 10: 31; John 2: 16; Mark 6: 56).

- **Skyscraper**:

Also see Tower, Ascend, Up, Mountain, Hills, and Elevator: Prophetic church of great revelation; high places; above earthly experience; higher spiritual things; Mt. Zion; sacrifice of worship; Mt. Sinai and the Ark of the Covenant in the Temple; Songs of ascent unto Him; Tower of Babel; Mt. Carmel; dominance; control; obstacle; Jesus returning from the heavens to earth; symbolic of victory; Jesus being lifted on the cross; wisdom that comes from above; Beatitudes in the Sermon on the Mount. (Acts 1: 13-14; 20: 7-8; Ps. 103: 11; 1 Sam. 9: 12-14; Matt 5; 1 Kings 18; John 3: 7; James 3: 15, 17; Heb. 1: 3; 1 Thess. 4: 13-18; 1 Kings 12: 31).

- **Trailer**:

Transitory and indefinite circumstances. (James 4: 14).

- **Vineyard**:

Jewish Nation; God's Kingdom; growing in grace; peace; fruitful wife or church; worthlessness. (Matt. 20: 1-6; Hos. 14: 7; John 15: 1-2, 6; Is. 5: 1-7; Ps. 128: 3; 1 Kings 4

Chapter 14

Dream Interpretation on Fruits

The meaning of fruit dreams is often positive, except on rare occasions where fruit dreams may come as a warning to the dreamer.

Fruits in dreams represent the gifts of God, the blessings of God, personal growth, prosperity, breakthrough, wealth, and all goodness.

FRUITS IN DREAMS SYMBOLIZE PRODUCTIVITY AND SUCCESS:

Genesis 1:28 KJV

And God blessed them, and said unto them, be fruitful, multiply, and replenish the earth, and subdue it: and have dominion over the fish of the sea, and over the fowl of the air, and over every living thing that moveth upon the earth.

When God commanded man to be fruitful, the instruction was for man to be productive and successful. If a man is unproductive, he fails woefully in his purpose for existence.

If you notice that the fruits in your dream are bad, it is time to sit up and pray hard. It's time to work hard. God hates laziness. Such dreams could also be a pointer to the enemy attacking your breakthrough and success.

Dream about Colors of Fruits:

Generally, fruit colors will relate to their natural colors. However, when they have a different original color. They could have hidden or implied meanings.

- **Black Fruit:** Black fruit in the dream means unexpected results.

- **Blue Fruit:** Blue fruits in the dream indicate that you must trust your wisdom and intuition.

- **Brown Fruit:** Brown fruits in the dream points to waiting too long. You missed your opportunity.

- **Yellow Fruit:** Yellow fruits promises fast healing to ill people.

- **Purple Fruit:** Purple fruits means that you will soon become royalty in some way.

- **White Fruit:** White fruits point to troubles with the mind.

- **Green Fruit:** Green fruits means immaturity.

Dream about Tastes of Fruits:

- **Sweet Juicy Ripe Fruit:** Sweet ripe, juicy fruit in the dream refers to plentiful and sweet fortune. You will enjoy richness and pleasure.

- **Sour Fruit:** Sour fruit in the dream means jealousy and missed opportunities. You will feel jealous of others who have made a profit with their work or investing choices. You have likely made your personal decisions hastily or prematurely. Thus you are expressing regrets about missed gains.

- **Fresh Fruit:** Fresh fruit in the dream means realizations on time. You can count on good timing and fortune. Enjoy your accomplishments. It is the best time to enjoy and indulge in your fruits of labor.

- **Unripe Fruit:** To dream about unripe fruits mean that you are too early with some decisions. Do not be so hasty about doing something. Take your time to let your knowledge and wisdom mature. You will be more experienced in taking on more advanced jobs.

DREAMING OF FRUITS ON A TREE:

The meaning of seeing fruits on a tree can be positive or negative, depending on the condition of the fruit. If the fruits are unripe, God works on something good in and for the dreamer. This calls for patience and cooperation on the part of the dreamer.

If the fruits are ripe, it is time to reap the fruits of your labor. God is set to bless you. There is a remarkable breakthrough coming your way.

Dream About Preparing Fruits:

- **Washing Fruit:** To see yourself washing fruits with water over a sink, point to a process of cleansing and growth. You will soon be getting over certain hard feelings with coworkers or colleagues.

- **Plucking or Picking Fruit:** Plucking fruits from trees or picking fruits from bushes in the dream; foretell richness and pleasure will become readily available. You will soon enjoy the fruit of your labor and love.

- **Cutting Fruit:** To dream of cutting open fruits with a knife; predicts that you will cut through your disillusions and apparent success. You will soon get to the core of your problems and successes. Perhaps you will redefine yourself by finding meaning underneath the surface.

- **Receiving Fruit:** To dream that you receive fruit from someone as a gift; foretells that someone will do you a critical favor. This favor will push you further in your success.

Personal Reflection

1. Have you ever seen fruit before in your dreams?

_____
_____
_____
_____
_____

2. Pray against every negative fruit dream?

_____
_____
_____
_____
_____

3. Claim the good ones you have by activating with the blood of Jesus Christ?

_____
_____
_____
_____
_____

Chapter 15

Power Against Midnight Raiders

The midnight hour is an hour of spiritual warfare. It is a night where the dark powers are gathered together to perpetrate their wickedness through dreams because they know that men are unconscious of what is going on in their environment during these hours.

The Bible says, while men slept, the enemy came to sow tares. The Bible has encouraged believers of this generation to be steadfast in prayers in season and out of season (Psalm 119:62). It is written in the Bible that God answers prayers at midnight hours. If believers of this generation must overcome their enemies, they must seriously take their night prayers within the hour of 1 am to 3 am.

One of the most powerful and yet the most important time to fight against the enemy is the midnight hours. The importance of midnight prayers plays meaningful effects on Christians who understand the power or mystery behind the midnight exercise.

Midnight prayer is a prayer done from midnight. It is the hour the enemy gathers together with their charms to fight against their victims. A wicked person can stand up at that hour to fire evil arrows. During midnight, people often encounter bad dreams and spiritual attacks on their bodies. The power of midnight is a battlefield between the believer and the devil. The common time for spiritual attacks is from 12 am -3 am

There are levels you can never attain in life without mastering the act of praying at midnight. Without midnight prayers, a person cannot obtain a total breakthrough or divine encounter with God in his dream. And there is no way a person can overcome his enemies without praying at midnight. It is sad but true that so many Christians are full of sleep.

Many believers have given the enemy full access to operating in their life. They have limited interest in midnight prayer warfare. During the sleep of many, demons have successfully sown many tares. The tares of backwardness, stagnation, failure at the edge of a breakthrough, sickness, poverty, late marriage, and others are suffering, confusion, mental attack, etc.

Jesus gave one illustration in the book of Matthew that a man went to his farm and planted good seeds and put some men there to guide it. But when the men started sleeping and did not do their work of being vigilant, the enemy came and sowed tares among the wheat and went his way. (Matthew 13:24,25).

This illustration has a lot of spiritual lessons. The watchmen were not vigilant or watchful, so the enemy came and planted evil seeds on the same farm! Spiritually speaking, for any Christian who is not vigilant and watchful or not a lover of midnight prayers, the devil will come and sow all manners of problems in their life.

That is why you see many Christian lives full of problems, obstacles, and setbacks, even though they are very committed to the Church, sowing seeds, and working for God. Why? Because they are full of sleep!

One clear divine sign is this;

If you are on the bed sleeping and you are rolling around your bed unnecessarily in the night, it could be a sign that God wants you to stand up and take some prayers. Because that hour could be the time, the enemy is working against you.

Sometimes you wake up in the Midnight, and you won't be able to sleep again, or you feel a touch in your body that wakes you up, or suddenly someone calls your name, and you wake up only to go back to sleep, and the voice says pray this are signs of God calling you to take charge in prayers.

Serious Christians don't sleep too much at the midnight hour. Real soldiers of Christ never get tired of taking midnight prayers.

Some years ago, a brother dreamed about his married car being tied down with a demonic woman after she stole it. This wicked woman began to use it to trade .he woke up not understanding with it meant then his marriage started having issues; when he shared this dream, I was led by the holy spirit to ask him to pray against that wicked strong woman who is a Night Raiders that raided his marriage to release the car of his marriage and everything that belongs to his wedding.

God gave him victories, and his marriage car was restored, which also brought about the physical restoration of his marriage from all storms that were affecting it.

These wicked night powers don't rest; they are always on evil assignment, so you must also be spiritually sensitive.

What happens at midnight time?

"The Midnight is full of wicked activities, and also, it is associated with devious activities:

- It is the time of the satanic conference.
- It is a time when the enemies meet to deliver their report.
- It is a time the enemy re-strategies.
- It is a time when the enemy takes decisions that affect people, including Christians.
- It is when the enemies renew their evil covenants.
- It is when the most aggressive curses are issued against people's lives.
- It is the time for the most potent satanic sacrifices.
- It is time the enemy does evil programming into people's life, marriage, home, career, and destiny.
- It is the time for reinforcement.

- It is time the enemy uses to steal and kill virtues and blessings.
- It is the time for evil to gather against Glory.
- It is time the enemy uses to initiate the evil covenant .etc.
- It is time for an evil move.
- It is covenant time for most coven gatherings.
- It is the time of handing over notes of days to workers of night.
- It is the time of spiritual manipulations.
- It is the time of intensive darkness.
- It is the time of the wickedness of the wicked attacks.

Ninety-five percent of the problems faced during the day are programmed, completed, and delivered at night hours. Most of the terrible things people experience during the day are demonic activities that have been programmed from 12 am to 3 am. These are the activities of the powers called Midnight Raiders.

This is one of the reasons why you must not use your night to play because our night remains the best time to pray for a victorious life.

Who are the night Raiders that operate in the Midnight?

Wondering spirit. The impersonating evil spirits can sometimes also be the spirit of the dead.

Forest demons that wander in the night. Moving from one place to the other.
Wicked personalities on evil assignments. These are ancestral spirits and satanic spies who go about to spy. The night eye monitoring forces that, most time, curse people's dreams. When you are in your house, and you hear the cry of an owl, or you see a wall gecko, spiders are evil spies Marine powers. These are the night Raiders that recruit people; familiar forces, witchcraft spirits, spirit spouses, etc.

They are:

- The night Raiders
- Witchcraft powers
- Sorcerers
- Enchanters
- Diviners
- Spirit wives, and husbands.

One brother shared a dream about how he's always been molested in the night by a spirit wife, and his wife also shared the same experience. This happens every night in their dreams, so I was led to ask them to seal up their house, repent from the sin of arguments and for them to seal up their own life before they sleep by the blood of Jesus and also start a night vigil from 1 am to 3 am.

Using some prophetic Bible verses listed below, the wife suddenly has a dream after prayers seeing men coming towards their house but as they tried to get it, these great iron gates prevented them. Coming in, they wanted to cut it, but it was not possible; she said they shouted that they had come to have sex with her, and she began to pray for power changes hand suddenly, and she could not find them since then she doesn't have the such dream again the husband also had something similar encounter that he shut some doors that were open in the house and clean the house by disposing of many dirty things and that the fire of

God rages against the spirit wife who always comes to have sex with him .they both were able to sleep without night readers coming to raid them and through this their marriage received a divine transformation.

- Satanic ministers
- Occultic powers
- Counterfeit or fake angels

- Spiritually armed robbers
- Powers of the moon that smite by night.
- Terror of the night
- The pestilence that walketh in darkness
- Demon idols
- Night caterers

They operate through the floating spirit, which is in charge of:

- Spirit of heaviness
- Spirit of sadness
- Spirit of death
- Spirit of dejection
- Spirit of discouragement
- Spirit of sleeplessness
- Spirit of self-pity
- Spirit of suicide
- Spirit of anger
- Spirit of stealing and robbery
- Spirit of gossip
- Spirit of hatred
- Spirit of murder
- Spirit of retaliation
- Spirit of violence
- Spirit of sexual perversion
- Spirit of false spiritualties

- Spirit of marine recruiters
- Spirit of harloting
- Spirit of masturbation
- Spirit of infirmity
- Spirit of agitation
- Spirit of worry
- Spirit of spiritual blindness
- Spirit of poverty
- Spirit of affliction

A brother said he had a dream that someone stole his briefcase that was full of money and some other documents, and he tried to find it, but he could not; when he work up, things started turning around against him at work and financially he became broke and within a little time he went from owning a house to renting a house this is the work of Night Raiders the spirit of stealing.

I pray for you, every conscious and unconscious appointment you have formed with the power of darkness; I terminate them now, in the name of Jesus.

Personal Reflection

What you need first to do:

- Always ask for the fire of the Holy Spirit upon your inner man for power against the powers of the night.
- Be on fire for God always
- Always pray
- Don't allow laziness
- Always speak in the heavenly tongues
- Take charge of the high places of your house by commanding fire of the Holy Spirit into the high places of your home against every demonic altar that might have been erected in the spiritual realm by night powers.

NOTE: Surrender your life to Jesus. (It is a nonnegotiable decision)

The desire that you must possess your possessions

Determine that you must withdraw your hands from their affairs
You close the doors of your life by the power in the blood of Jesus against midnight Raiders.

You must permanently seal up your home with the blood of Jesus Christ

Anoint your door post, windows, and four corners of your home at least once a week for purification and sanctification and to close your house against their evil activity.

It would help if you got read of anything in your home connected to the forces of darkness, be it symbols, crystals, strange songs, movies, clothes dedicated to powers of darkness, rings or body products, etc.

It would help if you asked the Holy Spirit to open your eyes to see whatever is in your home that is connected to Night Raiders.

You have to renounce any unconscious covenant or initiation that may stand as a legal entry for the night powers.

Turn your night to revival. 1 am to 3 am.

Read Psalm 24 for every ancient door that the Night powers are using as a legal entry into your dream, home, star your children's life to be closed and that the king of Glory to take over and that He has a man of war should fight and shield you with fire.

Isaiah 60 for the shekinah glory of God to overshadowed you against the power of the night

It is time to wake up and take charge of your night through the power of the Holy Spirit in this wicked and perverse generation. May you receive grace and divine understanding to become your prophet through the power of the Holy Spirit in Jesus' name.

Pray the kind of prayers we will pray now—part 1:

Psalm 91 ....confession

Powers of the night, attacking my destiny, affliction my life, projecting evil into my star at night, losing your hold, and dying in the name of Jesus.

Powers of the night, release my portion which you have stolen from me in the name of Jesus.
Satanic night caterers, night Raiders, I am not your candidate; die in the name of Jesus.

Arrows of the powers of the night backfire in the name of Jesus
Powers of the night of my father's house, powers of the night of my mother's house, you are a liar, be destroyed in the name of Jesus

Angels of war, hear the Word of the Lord, pursue my pursuers in the name of Jesus.

Any power is projecting evil into my destiny, destroyed by fire in the name of Jesus.

Pray and declare that by the fire of the Holy Ghost, you are fortified and shielded from every perfected plan of the devil against you. Declare that the plan shall not be executed in Jesus' name.

For I, saith the LORD, will be unto her a wall of fire round about and will be the Glory in the midst of her. (Zechariah 2:5, KJV)

Pray and declare that no plan by the devil against you will work even if they try to execute it; it will always fail, in Jesus' name.

Take counsel together, and it shall come to nought; speak the word, and it shall not stand: for God is with us. (Isaiah 8:10, KJV).

Pray and declare that any human agent of darkness that may be saddled with the responsibility for execution will be slain by the sword of God's angels, in Jesus' name.

Pray and bind spirit agents of Satan that may be saddled with the responsibility to execute, declare them immobile, in Jesus' name.

Behold, they shall surely gather together, but not by me: whosoever shall gather together against thee shall fall for thy sake. (Isaiah 54:15, KJV)
Pray and declare that you are covered and shielded by the blood of Jesus from every form of attack, in Jesus' name.

The LORD is our defense, and the Holy One of Israel is our king. (Psalm 89:18, KJV)
Pray and ask the Lord to guide your steps and always talk so that you will not foolishly fall into the hand of the enemy, in Jesus' name.

Part 2

Order my steps in thy word: and let not any iniquity have dominion over me. (Psalm 119:133, KJV):

1) Pray and receive cleansing by the blood of Christ from every sin that may open you up for the devil to succeed at attacking you, in Jesus' name.

2) I paralyze all the night caterers and forbid their food in my dream, in the name of Jesus.

3) All pursuers in my dreams, begin to pursue yourself in the name of Jesus.

4) I command my picture in the demonic kingdom, being used as a remote control against my life to burn into ashes, in Jesus' name.

5) I paralyze all the demonic delegates assigned to my life in the name of Jesus.

6) 1 total command destruction of all satanic technology against my life in the name of Jesus.

7) Every power of darkness hunting for my life, be roasted in the name of Jesus.

8) Let all the contamination in my life through dreams be cleansed by the blood of Jesus.

9) Let the path of the enemy into my life be permanently closed, in the name of Jesus.

10) Father Lord, fill my life with the Holy Ghost fire; I want to vomit fire in the name of Jesus.

11) I refuse to follow the evil prescription in the name of Jesus.

12) Let every evil thing done against me between the hours of 12 and 1 am be nullified, in the name of Jesus.

13) Let every evil thing doer- against me between the hours of 1 and 2 am be nullified, in the name of Jesus.

14) Let every evil thing done against me between the hours of 2 and 3 am be nullified, in the name of Jesus. 15. Let every evil thing done against me between the hours of 3 and . 4 am be nullified, in the name of Jesus.

15) I lose myself from all inherited bondage in the name of Jesus.

16) I vomit every satanic poison I have swallowed in Jesus' name.

17) Evil bands, release me in the name of Jesus.

18) I remove myself from every satanic bus stop, in Jesus' name.

19) I drink the blood of Jesus.

20) Let every owner of evil in my life begin to carry their loads in the name of Jesus.

21) I destroy every evil remote controlling power fashioned against me in the name of Jesus.

22) Holy Ghost fire, incubate my life.

23) I reverse every evil design fashioned against my life in the name of Jesus.

24) Every hidden or open spirit of infirmity, depart from my life, in the name of Jesus.

25) You evil strongman, be bound in the name of Jesus.

26) All evil authorities upon my life, I command you to break in the name of Jesus.

27) I remove my name from the book of backward steps in the name of Jesus.

28) 0 Lord, make my dream a prophetic dream in Jesus' name.

29) I take the two edged-sword of the spirit as my weapon and cut down the powers of darkness working against me in the hour. Of the night in Jesus' name.

30) Thank God for answering your prayers.

May the Lord God of Elijah answer you by fire in Jesus' name.

Chapter 16

Conclusion

Your dream that is talking about your destiny and glory which must manifest is your Joseph dream which can only be experienced through a mountain top life and also becoming a friend of God. In other for your Joseph dreams to manifest, bad dreams must be destroyed, and you must always walk according to his will.

Desire to be able to interpret your dream by yourself through the power of the Holy Spirit because there are ny people with whom you are not supposed to share your dream with, most time you can get an interpretation from People oppose what God is saying, but when you seek God's face and depend on him for interpretation, you will never miss it, and your future is secured and protected.

NOTE:

It is not everyone wrong; sometimes God may lead you to a certain person for you to get information and leading concerning what he has shown you.

Whatever you want to do, build a good relationship with God, be His friend like Abraham, and surrender your ways unto him. My prayer for you today is that your Joseph dream will surely manifest in the name of Jesus Christ.

Personal Reflection

1) Write out all the good dreams which are your Joseph dream in your journal?

_____

_____

_____

_____

_____

_____

_____

_____

2) Begin activating it by anointing yourself and praying to activate your Godly dream?

_____

_____

_____

_____

_____

_____

_____

_____

Made in the USA
Las Vegas, NV
22 September 2023